KRAFT HOLIDAY HOMECOMING™

© Copyright 1995 Kraft Foods, Inc.
© Copyright 1995 Meredith Corporation. All rights reserved. Printed in Hong Kong.
Produced by Meredith Custom Publishing, 1912 Grand Ave., Des Moines, Iowa 50309-3379.

Pictured on front cover (clockwise from bottom right):
Heavenly Chocolate Cake (recipe, page 52),
Chocolate Cherry Thumbprint Cookies (recipe, page 78),
ONE BOWL® Brownies (recipe, page 59).

Season's Greetings...

There's no more delightful holiday welcome than the aromas of our favorite foods coming from the kitchen. They're an enduring symbol of the traditions we share with those closest to us at this time of year. This book is dedicated to the holidays, to making each moment reflect a celebration of good food and warm hospitality.

In that spirit, we're proud to present to you this collection of delicious recipes. Made with ingredients from the *Family of Fine Food Products of Kraft Foods* and tested in our own Kraft Creative Kitchens, this selection of appetizers, main dishes, side dishes and salads, desserts and food gifts will ensure you a joyful holiday with all your family and friends.

In addition, you'll find dozens of useful hints and suggestions for making the season relaxing and memorable. For instance, you can prepare everything from a Thanksgiving potluck feast to a delectable cookie and candy exchange by following our special menu plans. Create pretty food presentations by using our simple garnishes. And bring your family and friends together in special celebrations with our series of "Share the Holidays" ideas.

All of us at Kraft Foods hope you'll find this *Holiday Homecoming*™ book helpful and inspirational as you share your hospitality this season. Happy holidays from our family to yours.

CONTENTS

A GALLERY OF
APPETIZERS AND
SNACKS

From elegant to homey, this
tasty collection of tiny bites,
fast-to-fix snacks and
make-ahead dips and
spreads is ideal for holiday
get-togethers. Made with
KRAFT® products, they com-
bine easy preparation with
sure success to give any
party a festive flavor.

Clockwise from lower left:
Chili Cheese Dip (recipe, page 12),
Festive Roasted Pepper Dip (recipe, page 8),
Ideas for Prepared Dips (tip, page 16),
Bacon-Cheddar Appetizers (recipe, page 24)

SHREDDED WHEAT PARTY MIX

When last-minute guests are coming over,
"bake" this popular snack mix in your microwave—
it takes only 6 minutes!

Prep time: 10 minutes
Baking time: 30 minutes OR
Microwave cooking time: 6 minutes

    4 cups NABISCO SPOON SIZE Shredded Wheat
    I cup popped popcorn
    I cup small unsalted pretzels
    3 tablespoons PARKAY Spread Sticks, melted
    I tablespoon Worcestershire sauce
    I teaspoon seasoned salt

I. Heat oven to 300°F.

2. Mix cereal, popcorn and pretzels in 15x10x1-inch baking pan. Mix PARKAY, Worcestershire sauce and seasoned salt in small bowl. Drizzle evenly over cereal mixture; toss to coat.

3. Bake 30 minutes or until crisp, stirring halfway through baking time. Cool. Store in tightly covered container.

Makes 12 (¹/₂-cup) servings.

To microwave: Mix cereal, popcorn and pretzels in large microwavable bowl. Mix remaining ingredients and toss to coat as directed at left.

• Microwave on HIGH 5 to 6 minutes or until crisp, stirring halfway through cooking time; cool. Store in tightly covered container.

Note: NABISCO is a registered trademark of Nabisco, Inc.

FESTIVE APPETIZER SPREAD

So easy, yet so elegant. Serve this tasty cheese spread
in a fancy mold or a plain shallow dish. Either way,
your guests will be impressed.

Prep time: 15 minutes plus refrigerating

    2 packages (8 ounces each) PHILADELPHIA BRAND Cream
        Cheese, softened
    I jar (8 ounces) CHEEZ WHIZ Pasteurized Process Cheese
        Sauce
    ¹/₄ cup *each* chopped red pepper and sliced green onions
    2 teaspoons Worcestershire sauce

I. Mix all ingredients with electric mixer on medium speed until well blended. Refrigerate.

2. Garnish with chopped nuts, parsley or fresh vegetable cutouts. Serve with assorted crackers, breads, breadsticks or cut-up vegetables.

Makes 2 cups.

DILLY DIP

*The delightful mix of dill, onion and parsley delivers an
irresistible dip that's simply heavenly with fresh veggies.*

Prep time: 5 minutes plus refrigerating

- 1 container (16 ounces) BREAKSTONE'S *or* KNUDSEN Sour Cream
- 1 cup MIRACLE WHIP *or* MIRACLE WHIP LIGHT Dressing
- 4 teaspoons *each* dill weed, instant minced onion and parsley flakes

1. Mix all ingredients. Refrigerate.

2. Serve with assorted cut-up vegetables.

Makes 3 cups.

FESTIVE ROASTED PEPPER DIP

*Light ingredients make this a healthful dip for the holidays
(photo, pages 4–5).*

Prep time: 10 minutes plus refrigerating

- 1 cup (8 ounces) BREAKSTONE'S Sour Cream *or* LIGHT CHOICE Sour Half & Half
- 1 cup KRAFT LIGHT Mayonnaise Dressing
- 1 jar (7½ ounces) roasted red peppers, drained, finely chopped
- 1 can (4 ounces) chopped green chilies, drained
- 1 tablespoon lemon juice
- ½ teaspoon garlic powder

1. Mix all ingredients. Refrigerate.

2. Serve with assorted cut-up vegetables.

Makes 3 cups.

RANCH DIP

*Bits of bacon give this dip a hearty, smoked flavor
that's excellent with vegetables or crackers.*

Prep time: 10 minutes plus refrigerating

    1 cup BREAKSTONE'S *or* KNUDSEN Sour Cream, any variety
    ½ cup KRAFT Ranch Dressing
    ¼ cup (1 ounce) KRAFT 100% Grated Parmesan Cheese
    4 slices OSCAR MAYER Bacon, crisply cooked, crumbled
    2 tablespoons sliced green onion

1. Mix all ingredients. Refrigerate.

2. Serve with assorted cut-up vegetables or crackers.

Makes about 1½ cups.

Note: If you like, substitute SEVEN SEAS VIVA Ranch
Dressing for KRAFT Ranch Dressing.

SHARE THE HOLIDAYS

Visit the homes of faraway relatives and friends via a video greeting featuring your
entire family. Just ask a neighbor to help with the camera chores. If you live in a
cold-weather climate, present yourselves building a snowman or selecting a tree
from a Christmas tree farm. If you're surrounded by balmy weather, tape your holiday message against a backdrop of poinsettias or blooming holly bushes. To share
your holiday video with more than one family member or friend, check your local
directory for businesses that can duplicate the tape inexpensively. Ship the copies in
mailers decorated with holiday stickers and stamps.

ITALIAN VEGETABLE DIP

This quick-to-fix dip saves on prep time by using a salad dressing mix as a shortcut seasoning blend.

Prep time: 10 minutes plus refrigerating

- 1 cup BREAKSTONE'S *or* KNUDSEN Sour Cream
- 1 cup KRAFT Real Mayonnaise
- 1 envelope GOOD SEASONS Zesty Italian Salad Dressing Mix
- ¼ cup finely chopped green pepper
- ¼ cup finely chopped red pepper

1. Mix sour cream, mayonnaise and salad dressing mix. Stir in green and red pepper. Refrigerate.

2. Serve with assorted cut-up vegetables, breadsticks, boiled potatoes or chips.

Makes 2¼ cups.

COOL CUCUMBER-DILL DIP

It's as easy as one, two—just stir a few ingredients into KRAFT Ranch Dressing to transform it into a refreshing dip.

Prep time: 10 minutes plus refrigerating

- 1 cup KRAFT Ranch Dressing
- ½ cup finely chopped, seeded, peeled cucumber
- 2 tablespoons finely chopped onion
- ½ teaspoon dill weed

1. Mix all ingredients. Refrigerate.

2. Serve with assorted cut-up vegetables, pita bread wedges and breadsticks.

Makes 1⅓ cups.

Italian Vegetable Dip
Savory Spinach Dip (recipe, page 14)

BACON-HORSERADISH DIP

*Worcestershire, horseradish and hot pepper sauce give this
dip its spicy appeal. If you like, prepare the dip ahead so
the flavors have plenty of time to blend.*

Prep time: 10 minutes plus refrigerating

1 container (16 ounces) BREAKSTONE'S *or* KNUDSEN
   Sour Cream
1 can (3 ounces) OSCAR MAYER Real Bacon Bits
1 tablespoon KRAFT Prepared Horseradish
1 tablespoon Worcestershire sauce
1/2 teaspoon hot pepper sauce
Dash garlic powder

1. Mix all ingredients. Refrigerate.

2. Serve with assorted cut-up vegetables, crackers
   or chips.

Makes 2¼ cups.

CHILI CHEESE DIP

*Perfect for entertaining, this zesty dip requires no last-minute
preparation. Simply heat it in the oven while you're welcoming your
guests, then set it out to warm up the party (photo, pages 4–5).*

Prep time: 5 minutes
Baking time: 25 minutes

1 package (8 ounces) PHILADELPHIA BRAND Cream
   Cheese, softened
1 can (15 ounces) chili without beans
1 cup (4 ounces) KRAFT Natural Shredded Sharp
   Cheddar Cheese

1. Heat oven to 350°F.

2. Spread cream cheese on bottom of 9-inch pie
   plate or quiche dish. Top with chili and cheddar
   cheese.

3. Bake 20 to 25 minutes or until thoroughly heated. Garnish with chopped green onion and tomato.
   Serve with tortilla chips.

Makes 8 to 10 servings.

VELVEETA® SALSA DIP

What could be easier than this smooth and spicy appetizer?
Keep these two ingredients on hand to turn any impromptu
gathering into a party.

Prep time: 5 minutes
Microwave cooking time: 5 minutes

- 1 pound **VELVEETA** Pasteurized Process Cheese Spread, cut up
- 1 jar (8 ounces) salsa

1. Microwave process cheese spread and salsa in 1½-quart microwavable bowl on HIGH 5 minutes or until process cheese spread is melted, stirring after 3 minutes.

2. Serve hot with assorted cut-up vegetables or tortilla chips.

Makes 3 cups.

SAVORY SPINACH DIP

*Made on the stove or in the microwave, this colorful dip is
ready to serve in just minutes (photo, page 10).*

Prep time: 5 minutes
Stovetop cooking time: 10 minutes OR
Microwave cooking time: 8 minutes

> 2 slices OSCAR MAYER Bacon, finely chopped
> 1/3 cup chopped red pepper
> 1 clove garlic, minced
> 1 package (10 ounces) frozen chopped spinach, cooked, well drained
> 1 jar (8 ounces) CHEEZ WHIZ Pasteurized Process Cheese Sauce
> 1/2 cup BREAKSTONE'S *or* KNUDSEN Sour Cream

1. Cook and stir bacon in saucepan on medium heat until crisp; drain. Add red pepper and garlic. Cook 1 minute or until tender.

2. Stir in remaining ingredients. Cook, stirring constantly, until thoroughly heated.

3. Serve with Italian bread cubes or assorted crackers.

Makes 2 cups.

To microwave: Microwave bacon in 1-quart microwavable bowl on HIGH 1 to 2 minutes or until crisp; drain.

• Stir in red pepper and garlic. Microwave 1 minute or until tender.

• Stir in remaining ingredients. Microwave on MEDIUM (50%) 4 to 5 minutes or until thoroughly heated, stirring every minute.

HOT ARTICHOKE DIP

*Make this dip and place it in a pretty quiche dish for an
elegant appetizer at any holiday gathering.*

Prep time: 10 minutes
Baking time: 20 minutes
Standing time: 5 minutes

> 1 can (14 ounces) artichoke hearts, drained, chopped
> 1 cup (4 ounces) KRAFT 100% Grated Parmesan Cheese
> 1 cup (4 ounces) KRAFT Natural Shredded Low-Moisture Part-Skim Mozzarella Cheese
> 3/4 cup KRAFT Real Mayonnaise *or* MIRACLE WHIP Salad Dressing
> 1 clove garlic, minced

1. Heat oven to 350°F.

2. Mix all ingredients. Spoon into 9-inch quiche dish *or* pie plate.

3. Bake 20 minutes. Let stand 5 minutes. Garnish with steamed artichoke leaves and red cabbage leaves.

4. Serve with toasted French bread slices or crackers.

Makes 2 cups.

Hot Artichoke Dip

PHILLY® 7-LAYER MEXICAN DIP

*For a reduced-fat version of this party favorite, use PHILADELPHIA BRAND
Neufchatel Cheese, ⅓ Less Fat than Cream Cheese or PHILADELPHIA BRAND
FREE Fat Free Cream Cheese instead of regular cream cheese.*

Prep time: 10 minutes plus refrigerating

1 package (8 ounces) **PHILADELPHIA BRAND** Cream Cheese, softened

1 tablespoon taco seasoning mix

1 cup prepared guacamole

1 cup salsa

1 cup shredded lettuce

1 cup (4 ounces) **KRAFT** Natural Shredded Sharp Cheddar Cheese

½ cup chopped green onions

2 tablespoons sliced pitted ripe olives

1. Mix cream cheese and seasoning mix. Spread on bottom of 9-inch pie plate or quiche dish.

2. Layer remaining ingredients over cream cheese mixture. Refrigerate.

3. Serve with tortilla chips.

Makes 6 to 8 servings.

IDEAS FOR PREPARED DIPS

Keep prepared **KRAFT** sour cream dips on hand so you'll always be ready to entertain on a moment's notice. You can find these dips in a variety of flavors in the dairy case at your local supermarket. To go beyond the classic duo of chips and dip, try these exciting ideas:

• Serve garlic bagel chips, breadsticks, toasted pita bread triangles, pretzel rods and big chewy pretzels for a new twist in dippers.

• Enhance the holiday crudité platter with sweet potato rounds, rutabaga and fennel slices, jicama and asparagus spears and Belgian endive leaves.

• Spoon **KRAFT** French Onion Dip into hollowed-out cherry tomatoes or steamed small, red potatoes.

• Serve your favorite **KRAFT** dip in containers such as hollowed-out round bread loaves, bell peppers, acorn squashes or small red or green cabbages.

KRAFT®
Creative Kitchens

CARBONARA APPETIZERS

Cook the bacon and chop the onion and parsley ahead of time.
Then when your guests arrive, just assemble, bake and serve.

Prep time: 15 minutes
Baking time: 8 minutes

 1 Italian bread shell (6 inches)
¼ cup DI GIORNO Alfredo Sauce
 2 slices OSCAR MAYER Bacon, crisply cooked, crumbled
 3 tablespoons chopped red onion
 2 teaspoons chopped fresh parsley
 2 teaspoons KRAFT 100% Grated Parmesan Cheese

1. Heat oven to 450°F.

2. Spread bread shell with sauce; layer with remaining ingredients.

3. Bake on ungreased cookie sheet 8 minutes or until bread shell is crisp and thoroughly heated. Cut into wedges.

Makes 6 servings.

PARTY PIZZA APPETIZERS

These mini pizzas are not only delicious to eat, but fun to
make. For a party activity, have each guest assemble his or
her own pizza, then bake and enjoy.

Prep time: 10 minutes
Baking time: 10 minutes

 1 can (10 ounces) refrigerated flaky buttermilk biscuits
½ cup pizza sauce
 1 cup (4 ounces) KRAFT Natural Shredded Low-Moisture Part-Skim Mozzarella Cheese
¼ cup finely chopped green pepper
   Dried oregano leaves

1. Heat oven to 450°F.

2. Separate biscuits on greased cookie sheet. Flatten each biscuit with bottom of greased glass.

3. Top biscuits with pizza sauce and cheese. Sprinkle with green pepper and oregano.

4. Bake 8 to 10 minutes or until cheese is melted.

Makes 10.

PARTY CHEESE WREATH

*This pretty wreath will add a festive touch to your holiday
table. If you like, assemble and garnish it ahead of time.
When your guests arrive, add the crackers and serve.*

Prep time: 15 minutes plus refrigerating

- 2 packages (8 ounces each) PHILADELPHIA BRAND Cream
  Cheese, softened
- 1 package (8 ounces) KRAFT Natural Shredded Mild Cheddar
  Cheese
- 1 tablespoon *each* chopped red bell pepper and finely
  chopped green onion
- 2 teaspoons Worcestershire sauce
- 1 teaspoon lemon juice
  Dash ground red pepper

1. Beat cream cheese and cheddar cheese with
electric mixer on medium speed until well blended.

2. Add remaining ingredients; mix well. Refrigerate
several hours.

3. Place drinking glass, about 3 inches in diameter,
in center of serving platter. Drop rounded tablespoonfuls of mixture around glass, just touching
outer edge of glass to form ring; smooth with spatula. Remove glass. Garnish with chopped parsley and
red bell pepper. Serve with assorted crackers.

Makes 2 cups.

REFRESHING CUCUMBER,
DILL 'N' CHEDDAR SNACKS

*Simple to make, these tasty tidbits require no cooking; just
assemble them right before your party.*

Assorted crackers

Cucumber slices

CRACKER BARREL Sharp Natural Cheddar Cheese, thinly
sliced and cut into shapes with cookie cutters

Fresh dill sprigs

Top each cracker with a cucumber slice, cheese
and dill sprig.

Party Cheese Wreath

QUICK CRABMEAT APPETIZER

*Arrange a variety of crackers or party breads around this
colorful spread for an eye-catching presentation.*

Prep time: 5 minutes

- 1 package (8 ounces) PHILADELPHIA BRAND Cream Cheese,
  softened
- ¼ cup SAUCEWORKS Cocktail Sauce
- 1 package (8 ounces) imitation crabmeat *or* 1 package
  (6 ounces) frozen cooked tiny shrimp, thawed, drained

1. Spread cream cheese on serving plate.

2. Pour cocktail sauce over cream cheese; top with
imitation crabmeat.

3. Serve with crackers or cocktail rye bread slices.

Makes 6 to 8 servings.

CHEDDAR AND ONION BITES

These bite-size snacks take just minutes to prepare (photo, page 23).

Prep time: 10 minutes
Broiling time: 3 minutes

- ⅓ cup KRAFT Real Mayonnaise
- 2 tablespoons chopped green onion
- 16 slices cocktail rye bread, toasted
- 1 package (10 ounces) CRACKER BARREL Sharp Natural Cheddar
  Cheese, thinly sliced

1. Heat broiler.

2. Mix mayonnaise and onion; spread on toasted
bread slices. Top with cheese. Place on cookie
sheet.

3. Broil 2 to 3 minutes or until cheese is melted.
Garnish as desired.

Makes 16.

Note: If you like, substitute rye crackers for toasted
cocktail rye bread.

CHEESE AND PESTO TOASTS

*The combination of pesto and sharp cheddar cheese gives
these toasted snacks extra flavor.*

Prep time: 10 minutes
Broiling time: 3 minutes

½ cup prepared pesto sauce

15 slices Italian bread, lightly toasted

30 slices plum tomato (about 5 medium tomatoes)

1 package (10 ounces) CRACKER BARREL Extra Sharp
Natural Cheddar Cheese, thinly sliced

1. Heat broiler.

2. Spread pesto sauce on toasted bread slices. Top
each toast slice with 2 tomato slices and 1 cheese
slice. Place on cookie sheet.

3. Broil 2 to 3 minutes or until cheese is melted.

Makes 15.

SHARE THE HOLIDAYS

Make the 12 days of Christmas a joyful memory for a special person in your life. Simply
purchase or make a dozen inexpensive gifts, then leave one in an out-of-the-way place on
each day leading up to Christmas. If you like, you can take your cues from the traditional
song and find gifts that relate to each day—give a jump rope for "lords a-leaping" or a
colorful tin of holiday cookies and a carton of milk for "maids a-milking."

CINNAMON 'N' APPLE WAFERS

*Apples, crackers, cheese and a sweet coating lend delightful
flavor to this soon-to-be-favorite finger food.*

Prep time: 15 minutes
Baking time: 5 minutes

½ cup sugar
½ teaspoon ground cinnamon
¼ teaspoon ground nutmeg
1 *each* small red and green apple, thinly sliced
28 shredded whole wheat wafer crackers
1 package (10 ounces) CRACKER BARREL Vermont Sharp-
   White Natural Cheddar Cheese, thinly sliced

1. Heat oven to 350°F.

2. Mix sugar, cinnamon and nutmeg; toss with
apples. Place wafers on cookie sheet; top each with
1 cheese slice and 2 apple slices.

3. Bake 4 to 5 minutes or until cheese is melted.
Serve warm.

Makes 28.

TOASTED CHEESE WEDGES

*These savory cheese bites are usually deep-fat fried. For an
easier, no-mess method, we used the broiler instead.*

Prep time: 10 minutes
Broiling time: 3 minutes

1 package (10 ounces) CRACKER BARREL NEW YORK AGED
   RESERVE Natural Extra Sharp Cheddar Cheese
½ cup Italian-style bread crumbs
½ teaspoon crushed red pepper (optional)
1 egg, beaten

1. Heat broiler. Spray cookie sheet with no stick
cooking spray.

2. Cut cheese into ½-inch slices; cut slices diagonally in half. Mix bread crumbs and pepper. Dip
cheese in egg; coat with crumb mixture. Place on
prepared cookie sheet.

3. Broil 2 to 3 minutes or until cheese is melted.
Serve warm with pizza or spaghetti sauce, if
desired.

Makes 20.

Cheddar and Onion Bites (recipe, page 20)
Cinnamon 'n' Apple Wafers

BACON WATER CHESTNUTS

A sweet-and-tangy sauce makes these hot-out-of-the-oven snacks absolutely irresistible.

Prep time: 20 minutes
Baking time: 45 minutes

- 1 package (8 ounces) OSCAR MAYER Bacon, cut in half crosswise
- 1 can (8 ounces) whole water chestnuts, drained
- ½ cup MIRACLE WHIP *or* MIRACLE WHIP LIGHT Dressing
- ½ cup firmly packed brown sugar
- ¼ cup chili sauce

1. Heat oven to 350°F.

2. Cook bacon in large skillet on medium heat until almost crisp; drain. Wrap bacon around water chestnuts; secure with toothpicks. Place in baking dish.

3. Mix remaining ingredients; pour over water chestnuts.

4. Bake 45 minutes.

Makes about 24.

BACON-CHEDDAR APPETIZERS

Save on last-minute preparation by stirring together the topping ahead of time. Then, during your party, all you need to do is top the toast and broil (photo, pages 4–5).

Prep time: 20 minutes
Broiling time: 3 minutes

- 1 package (8 ounces) KRAFT Natural Shredded Sharp Cheddar Cheese
- 1 package (8 ounces) OSCAR MAYER Bacon, crisply cooked, crumbled
- ¼ cup KRAFT Real Mayonnaise
- 2 tablespoons finely chopped onion
- ½ teaspoon dry mustard
  Melba toast rounds

1. Heat broiler.

2. Mix all ingredients except toast rounds until well blended. Spread 1 teaspoon cheese mixture on each toast round. Place on cookie sheet.

3. Broil 2 to 3 minutes or until cheese is melted. Garnish as desired.

Makes about 5 dozen.

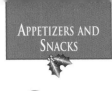

LITTLE GEMS

*An unusual combination of flavors creates a
delightful sauce for cocktail franks. Keep toothpicks or forks
nearby so guests can help themselves.*

Prep time: 5 minutes
Cooking time: 10 minutes

1 package (16 ounces) OSCAR MAYER Little Wieners
1 jar (12 ounces) chili sauce
1 jar (10 ounces) KRAFT Grape Jelly
2 tablespoons cornstarch

1. Heat wieners as directed on package.

2. Meanwhile, mix chili sauce, jelly and cornstarch in small saucepan. Cook on medium heat 5 minutes or until sauce thickens and boils, stirring frequently.

3. To serve, place wieners and sauce in slow cooker or fondue pot. Keep warm on low heat.

Makes about 50.

IDEAS FOR
LITTLE WIENERS AND LITTLE SMOKIES

Little Wieners and Little Smokies are bite-size versions of the regular OSCAR MAYER Wieners and Smokie Links. Serve them as appetizers and snacks or in main dishes. Here are just a few suggestions on how you can enjoy these tiny delicious treats.

- Heat them in a prepared sauce, such as bottled barbecue sauce, canned cheese soup or hot mustard. Serve them with decorative toothpicks for an uncomplicated appetizer.

- Heat and serve them in small dinner rolls or tiny buns made for mini hot dogs.

- Wrap each of them in refrigerated biscuit dough and bake.

- Add them to baked beans, macaroni and cheese, and other casserole dishes for added flavor and protein.

- Add them cold to salads, such as potato salad or Caesar salad.

KRAFT
Creative
Kitchens

LITTLE TACOS

The south-of-the-border essence comes from taco sauce.
Keep these Little Smokies warm in a fondue pot or slow cooker.

Prep time: 5 minutes
Cooking time: 10 minutes

- 1 package (16 ounces) OSCAR MAYER Little Smokies
- 1 jar (8 ounces) CHEEZ WHIZ Pasteurized Process Cheese Sauce
- ½ cup taco sauce

1. Heat smokies as directed on package.

2. Meanwhile, mix process cheese sauce and taco sauce in small saucepan. Cook on medium-low heat 10 minutes or until process cheese sauce melts, stirring frequently.

3. To serve, place smokies and sauce in fondue pot or slow cooker. Garnish with chopped fresh cilantro or parsley. Keep warm on low heat.

Makes about 50.

CATALINA® CHICKEN WINGS

When serving a crowd, you can marinate these favorites
ahead of time, then cook them to perfection just
before or during the party.

Prep time: 5 minutes plus marinating
Baking time: 45 minutes OR
Grilling time: 20 minutes OR
Broiling time: 20 minutes

- 1 bottle (16 ounces) KRAFT CATALINA French Dressing
- ½ cup soy sauce
- 5 pounds chicken wings, separated at joints, tips discarded, *and/or* chicken drummettes

1. Mix dressing and soy sauce; reserve ½ cup of the dressing mixture.

2. Pour remaining dressing mixture over chicken; cover. Refrigerate several hours or overnight to marinate. Drain; discard marinade.

3. Heat oven to 375°F.

4. Place chicken in 15x10x1-inch foil-lined baking pan. Bake 45 minutes or until golden brown, brushing halfway through baking with reserved ½ cup dressing mixture. Serve with blue cheese dressing sprinkled with cracked pepper.

Makes about 6 dozen.

To grill: Place chicken on grill over medium coals. Grill 20 minutes or until cooked through, turning once and brushing occasionally with reserved ½ cup dressing mixture.

To broil: Place chicken on broiler pan. Broil 6 inches from heat 20 minutes, turning once and brushing occasionally with reserved ½ cup dressing mixture.

SIDE TRIMMINGS

You can rely on these no-fuss accompaniments from Kraft Foods to dress up your holiday meals. This enticing assortment of salads, vegetable dishes, stuffings and rice pilafs includes everything from a new-fashioned Honey Dijon Waldorf Salad to Classic Green Bean Casserole.

Clockwise from left:
Favorite Spinach Salad
(recipe, page 40),
VELVEETA® Vegetable Bake
(recipe, page 35),
Brown Rice Almondine
(recipe, page 30)

SAUSAGE STUFFING

This versatile stuffing is incredible on its own or stuffed in a chicken or turkey (photos, below and on page 90).

Prep time: 10 minutes
Cooking time: 10 minutes
Standing time: 5 minutes

¼   pound bulk pork sausage
1   cup sliced celery
1   cup sliced mushrooms
     (about ¼ pound)
1   small onion, chopped
1½   cups beef broth
1   teaspoon poultry seasoning
½   teaspoon salt
1½   cups MINUTE Original
     or Premium Long Grain
     Rice, uncooked

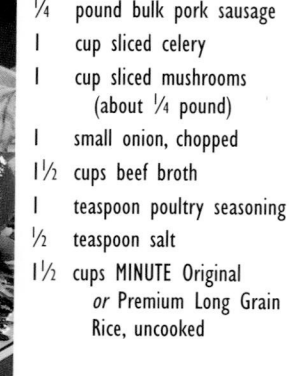

1. Brown sausage in saucepan or skillet on medium-high heat. Add celery, mushrooms and onion; cook and stir 3 minutes.

2. Stir in broth, seasoning and salt. Bring to boil. Stir in rice; cover. Remove from heat.

3. Let stand 5 minutes.

Makes about 5 cups stuffing or 10 servings.

Roasted Chicken with Sausage Stuffing:
Prepare stuffing as directed. Spoon into 4½- to 5-pound roasting chicken. Do not pack tightly. Roast at once as directed on poultry wrapper.

Note: Stuffing recipe can be doubled or tripled for turkey.

BROWN RICE ALMONDINE

Perfect for the holidays and year-round (photo, pages 28–29).

Prep time: 10 minutes
Microwave cooking time: 10 minutes
Standing time: 5 minutes

1½ cups MINUTE Instant Brown Rice, uncooked
1¼ cups chicken broth
1 medium onion, chopped
1 tablespoon lemon juice
1 tablespoon PARKAY Spread Sticks
2 teaspoons chopped fresh dill or ½ teaspoon dill weed
1 clove garlic, minced
1 cup frozen cut green beans, thawed
2 tablespoons toasted sliced almonds

1. Mix rice, broth, onion, juice, PARKAY, dill and garlic in 2-quart microwavable casserole; cover.

2. Microwave on HIGH 5 minutes. Stir in beans; cover.

3. Microwave 5 minutes. Let stand 5 minutes. Stir in almonds. Garnish with lemon slices and additional fresh dill.

Makes 6 servings.

BROWN RICE AND CRANBERRY PILAF

*When you're searching for something special to go with your
main dish, look no further. This moist and colorful pilaf is a
wonderful alternative to plain rice.*

Prep time: 5 minutes
Cooking time: 10 minutes
Standing time: 5 minutes

- 2 cups chicken broth
- 1 cup orange juice
- 3 cups MINUTE Instant Brown Rice, uncooked
- 1 cup fresh cranberries *or* 1 cup whole berry cranberry sauce
- ¼ cup sliced almonds, toasted

1. Bring broth and juice to boil.

2. Stir in rice and cranberries. Return to boil.
Reduce heat to low; cover and simmer 5 minutes.
Remove from heat.

3. Let stand 5 minutes. Stir in almonds.

Makes 10 servings.

SHARE THE HOLIDAYS

Cheer up the older people in your neighborhood who will be alone during the holidays
by designating them as honorary grandparents. Take them with you to a school pageant
or concert, and invite them to share in your family festivities. If they're confined because
of a disability or lack of transportation, treat them to the sights and sounds of the holidays
by decorating their home or driving them downtown to see the storefront decorations or
other seasonal attractions.

VELVEETA® CHEESY RICE AND BROCCOLI

*Delicious with poultry, pork or beef or by itself as a
meatless entrée, this hearty dish will soon become a family
favorite for the holiday season and throughout the year.*

Prep time: 5 minutes
Cooking time: 10 minutes
Standing time: 10 minutes

1 package (10 ounces) frozen chopped broccoli, thawed,
drained
1 cup water
1½ cups MINUTE Original Rice, uncooked
½ pound VELVEETA Pasteurized Process Cheese Spread
or VELVEETA LIGHT Pasteurized Process Cheese Product,
cut up

1. Bring broccoli and water to full boil in medium
saucepan on medium-high heat.

2. Add rice; cover and remove from heat. Let
stand 4 to 5 minutes.

3. Stir in process cheese spread. Cover and let
stand 4 to 5 minutes. Stir until process cheese
spread is melted before serving.

Makes 6 servings.

HERB-ROASTED POTATOES

*For a colorful potato dish, we suggest using red-skinned potatoes. If the smaller
potatoes are unavailable, then use larger ones and cut each into six or eight pieces.*

½ cup MIRACLE WHIP Salad Dressing
1 tablespoon *each* dried oregano leaves, garlic powder and
onion powder
1 teaspoon seasoned salt
1 tablespoon water
2 pounds small red potatoes, quartered

1. Heat oven to 425°F.

2. Mix dressing, seasonings and water in large
bowl. Add potatoes; toss to coat. Place potatoes on
greased cookie sheet.

3. Bake 20 minutes. Turn potatoes; continue
baking 20 minutes or until crisp and browned.

Makes 8 servings.

Prep time: 15 minutes
Baking time: 40 minutes

VELVEETA® Cheesy Rice and Broccoli

QUICK CHEESY MASHED POTATOES

The secret to these golden, delicious potatoes is the VELVEETA Cheese Spread. Cut the cheese spread into tiny cubes so the hot potatoes can melt it easily.

Prep time: 20 minutes

  4 cups hot cooked sliced potatoes
½ pound **VELVEETA** Pasteurized Process Cheese Spread, cut up
    Salt and pepper

1. Mash potatoes coarsely with fork or potato masher.

2. Add process cheese spread. Mash until process cheese spread is melted and potatoes are desired consistency.

3. Season to taste with salt and pepper.

Makes 6 servings.

PRALINE SWEET POTATOES

Flavored with brown sugar, cinnamon and pecans, these luscious potatoes will become a new tradition for your family Thanksgiving dinners.

Prep time: 45 minutes
Baking time: 30 minutes

  2 pounds sweet potatoes, cooked, peeled and mashed
½ cup **MIRACLE WHIP** Salad Dressing
½ cup firmly packed brown sugar, divided
  1 teaspoon ground ginger
¼ teaspoon grated orange peel
¼ cup chopped pecans
  1 tablespoon **PARKAY** Spread Sticks, softened
¼ teaspoon ground cinnamon

1. Heat oven to 350°F.

2. Mix sweet potatoes, salad dressing, ¼ cup of the sugar, ginger and peel. Spoon into 1½-quart casserole.

3. Mix remaining ¼ cup sugar, pecans, **PARKAY** and cinnamon; sprinkle over potato mixture.

4. Bake 30 minutes.

Makes 8 servings.

VELVEETA® VEGETABLE BAKE

Let your imagination go and create your own signature dish. We suggest using broccoli, but any frozen vegetable would be impressive in this cheesy casserole (photo, pages 28–29).

Prep time: 5 minutes
Baking time: 30 minutes

- 1 package (16 ounces) frozen broccoli cuts, partially cooked, drained
- ¾ pound **VELVEETA** Pasteurized Process Cheese Spread, cut up
- ¾ cup crushed buttery crackers
- 2 tablespoons **PARKAY** Spread Sticks

1. Heat oven to 375°F.

2. Mix broccoli and process cheese spread. Spoon into greased 1½-quart casserole. Sprinkle with crushed crackers; dot with PARKAY.

3. Bake 25 to 30 minutes or until thoroughly heated.

Makes 4 to 6 servings.

SPINACH LASAGNA

This extraordinary lasagna can be served as a substantial side dish or as a meatless entrée.

Prep time: 30 minutes
Baking time: 45 minutes
Standing time: 10 minutes

- 1 container (15 ounces) ricotta cheese *or* cottage cheese
- 1 package (10 ounces) frozen chopped spinach, thawed, well drained
- 3 cups (12 ounces) **KRAFT** Natural Shredded Low-Moisture Part-Skim Mozzarella Cheese, divided
- ¾ cup (3 ounces) **KRAFT** 100% Grated Parmesan Cheese, divided
- 2 eggs, beaten
- 1 jar (28 ounces) spaghetti sauce, divided
- 9 lasagna noodles, cooked, drained

1. Heat oven to 350°F.

2. Mix ricotta cheese, spinach, 2 cups of the mozzarella cheese, ½ cup of the Parmesan cheese and eggs.

3. Layer 1 cup of the spaghetti sauce, 3 lasagna noodles and ½ of the ricotta cheese mixture in 13x9-inch baking dish. Repeat layers. Top with remaining 3 noodles, 1 cup sauce, 1 cup mozzarella and ¼ cup Parmesan cheese.

4. Bake 45 minutes. Let stand 10 minutes before serving.

Makes 8 to 10 servings.

BACON BREAKFAST CASSEROLE

*Serve this make-ahead main dish with coffee cake
and fruit for a festive wake-up call.*

Prep time: 20 minutes plus refrigerating
Baking time: 1 hour
Standing time: 10 minutes

- 8 slices white bread, crusts trimmed
- 8 slices OSCAR MAYER Bacon, crisply cooked, crumbled
- 1 can (4 ounces) sliced mushrooms, drained
- 2 green onions, sliced
- 1½ cups (6 ounces) KRAFT Natural Shredded Mild Cheddar Cheese
- 4 eggs, beaten
- 2 cups milk

1. Place 4 bread slices on bottom of greased 8-inch square baking dish. Sprinkle bacon, mushrooms, onions and cheese on bread. Cover with remaining 4 bread slices.

2. Mix eggs and milk; pour over bread. Cover. Refrigerate 1 hour or overnight.

3. Heat oven to 350°F.

4. Bake, uncovered, 1 hour. Let stand 10 minutes before serving. Garnish as desired.

Makes 6 servings.

SHARE THE HOLIDAYS

Children appreciate a day of their own. During the holiday season, designate a day to honor each child in your family. On the special day, allow the honoree to choose the meal menus and to sit at the head of the table. Let the child select a holiday video or story or an activity the whole family can enjoy together. You also might want to ask the child's best friend to share in the fun.

Bacon Breakfast Casserole
Greens with Pear and Pecan (recipe, page 39)

CRANBERRY CREAM CHEESE MOLD

This refreshing salad adds a splash of color to any holiday meal. Serve it
as a mold or sliced on lettuce leaves (photos, below and on page 90).

Prep time: 30 minutes plus refrigerating

1½ cups boiling water

1 package (8-serving size) *or* 2 packages (4-serving size each) JELL-O Brand Cranberry Flavor Gelatin *or* Cranberry Flavor Sugar Free Low Calorie Gelatin Dessert *or* any red flavor

1½ cups cold water

½ teaspoon ground cinnamon

1 medium apple, chopped

1 cup whole berry cranberry sauce (optional)

1 package (8 ounces) PHILADELPHIA BRAND Cream Cheese *or* PHILADELPHIA BRAND Neufchatel Cheese, ⅓ Less Fat than Cream Cheese, softened

1. Stir boiling water into gelatin in large bowl 2 minutes or until completely dissolved. Stir in cold water and cinnamon.

2. Pour 2 cups of the gelatin into medium bowl. Refrigerate about 1½ hours or until thickened (spoon drawn through leaves a definite impression). Reserve remaining 1 cup gelatin at room temperature.

3. Stir apple and cranberry sauce into thickened gelatin. Spoon into 6-cup mold. Refrigerate about 30 minutes or until set but not firm (should stick to your finger when touched and should mound).

4. Stir reserved 1 cup gelatin gradually into cream cheese in small bowl with wire whisk until smooth. Pour over gelatin layer in mold.

5. Refrigerate 4 hours or until firm. Unmold. Garnish as desired. Store leftover gelatin mold in refrigerator.

Makes about 6 cups or 12 servings.

To unmold: Dip mold in hot water for about 15 seconds. Gently pull gelatin from around edges with moist fingers. Place moistened serving plate on top of mold. Invert mold and plate; holding mold and plate together, shake slightly to loosen. Gently remove mold and center gelatin on plate.

CLASSIC GREEN BEAN CASSEROLE

An all-time favorite, this version is better than ever with
CHEEZ WHIZ Process Cheese Sauce (photos, below and on page 90).

Prep time: 5 minutes
Baking time: 35 minutes

- 3 packages (9 ounces each) frozen French cut green beans, thawed, drained
- 1 jar (8 ounces) CHEEZ WHIZ Pasteurized Process Cheese Sauce
- 1 can (10¾ ounces) condensed cream of mushroom soup
- ⅛ teaspoon pepper
- 1 can (2.8 ounces) French fried onions, divided

1. Heat oven to 350°F.

2. Mix all ingredients except ½ can onions in 1½-quart casserole.

3. Bake 30 minutes. Top with remaining onions; continue baking 5 minutes. Garnish with red pepper cutouts or strips.

Makes 8 servings.

To make ahead: Prepare as directed except for baking; cover. Refrigerate overnight. When ready to serve, bake, uncovered, at 350°F for 45 to 50 minutes or until thoroughly heated, topping with remaining onions during last 5 minutes of baking time.

GREENS WITH PEAR AND PECAN

This flavorful salad looks elegant but is actually simple to prepare.
For variety, try a mixture of baby greens instead of the romaine
(photo, page 36).

Prep time: 20 minutes

- 6 cups torn romaine *or* leaf lettuce
- 2 medium pears, sliced
- 1 cup seedless red grapes
  KRAFT Ranch Dressing
- ⅓ cup pecan halves

1. Toss lettuce, pears and grapes in large bowl.

2. Just before serving, drizzle with dressing and sprinkle with pecans.

Makes 6 servings.

FAVORITE SPINACH SALAD

Filled with the crunch of water chestnuts and the flavor of hard-cooked eggs and bacon, this traditional spinach salad complements any meal (photo, pages 28–29).

Prep time: 15 minutes

5 cups torn spinach
2 cups sliced mushrooms
1 can (8 ounces) sliced water chestnuts, drained
1 cup bean sprouts
½ cup thinly sliced red onion wedges
4 slices OSCAR MAYER Bacon, crisply cooked, crumbled
2 hard-cooked eggs, chopped
¾ cup KRAFT CATALINA French Dressing

1. Toss all ingredients except dressing in large bowl.

2. Serve with dressing.

Makes 6 servings.

ITALIAN PASTA SALAD

Cool and refreshing, with robust Italian flavor, this salad is almost a meal in itself.

Prep time: 20 minutes plus refrigerating

1 package (16 ounces) pasta, cooked, drained
1 bottle (16 ounces) KRAFT Zesty Italian Dressing
1 cup *each* chopped green pepper, sliced pepperoni and sliced pitted ripe olives
½ cup (2 ounces) KRAFT 100% Grated Parmesan Cheese
2 teaspoons dried oregano leaves

1. Toss all ingredients in large bowl. Refrigerate.

Makes 12 servings.

*Italian Pasta Salad
Cheesey Biscuits (recipe, page 43)*

BACON-BROCCOLI SALAD

*Both totable and tasty, this spinach, broccoli and bacon salad
is sure to be a winner at your next holiday potluck.*

Prep time: 20 minutes plus refrigerating

1 cup MIRACLE WHIP Salad Dressing
2 tablespoons sugar

2 tablespoons vinegar
1 medium bunch broccoli, cut into flowerets
   (about 6 cups)
4 cups loosely packed torn spinach
12 slices OSCAR MAYER Bacon, crisply cooked, crumbled
½ cup slivered red onion
¼ cup raisins

1. Mix salad dressing, sugar and vinegar in large bowl.

2. Add remaining ingredients; mix lightly. Refrigerate.

Makes 8 servings.

HONEY DIJON WALDORF SALAD

*The classic Waldorf takes a twist with Honey Dijon
Dressing for a light, yet tangy, flavor.*

Prep time: 10 minutes plus refrigerating

2 cups chopped apples
½ cup KRAFT Honey Dijon Dressing
½ cup sliced celery
½ cup raisins
¼ cup chopped walnuts

Toss all ingredients in large bowl. Refrigerate.

Makes 4 servings.

CHEESY BISCUITS

Refrigerated biscuits take on the charming shape of a Christmas tree for a no-fuss holiday presentation. If you like, after baking the biscuit tree, place purchased bread-sticks at its base to fashion a trunk (photo, page 41).

Prep time: 10 minutes
Baking time: 10 minutes

- 1 jar (8 ounces) CHEEZ WHIZ Pasteurized Process Cheese Sauce
- 1 can (10 ounces) refrigerated buttermilk biscuits
- ½ cup (2 ounces) KRAFT 100% Grated Parmesan Cheese
  Dried herbs, such as parsley, basil, rosemary *or* oregano (optional)

1. Heat oven to 400°F.

2. Microwave process cheese sauce as directed on label; pour into small bowl.

3. Dip each biscuit top in process cheese sauce, then in Parmesan cheese, coating tops of rolls completely. Place biscuits, almost touching, on ungreased cookie sheet in the shape of a tree. Sprinkle with herbs.

4. Bake 8 to 10 minutes or until golden brown. Use a spatula to carefully transfer tree to large serving platter.

Makes 10 biscuits.

CHEESE AND TOMATO BREAD

An open-face stack of salad dressing, tomato and cheese, this side dish easily can be made to serve a crowd.

French bread slices
KRAFT House Italian with Olive Oil Blend Dressing
Plum tomato slices
KRAFT Natural Cheese Slices, cut in half diagonally

1. Heat broiler.

2. Place bread slices on cookie sheet. Broil until lightly browned. Brush toasted side of bread slices with dressing. Layer tomato and cheese slices on bread.

3. Broil until cheese is melted. Garnish with fresh basil.

SIMPLE 'N' SWEET

The holidays just wouldn't be the same without the home-baked goodness of decadent desserts. Now you can create those popular holiday flavors even if you're short on time, thanks to this merry assortment of cakes, pies and other tempting desserts.

Clockwise from top right: PHILLY 3-STEP™ Pumpkin Cheesecake (recipe, page 57), Creamy Chocolate Layered Pie (recipe, page 47), Brandied Coffee and French Coffee (recipes, page 55)

TEMPTING RASPBERRY TARTS

While children will love having their own sweet tarts, these individual desserts are elegant enough for a grown-up gathering.

Prep time: 10 minutes plus refrigerating

¼ cup honey

1 package (8 ounces) PHILADELPHIA BRAND Cream Cheese, softened

1 package (10 ounces) frozen red raspberries in light syrup, partially thawed, undrained

1 cup sliced banana

2 cups KRAFT Miniature Marshmallows

1¾ cups thawed COOL WHIP Whipped Topping

2 packages (4 ounces each) graham cracker tart shells (12 shells)

1. Add honey to cream cheese, mixing until well blended.

2. Stir in fruit. Gently stir in marshmallows and whipped topping.

3. Pour into shells. Refrigerate several hours or overnight. Garnish with fresh raspberries, mint leaves and additional marshmallows.

Makes 12 servings.

Tempting Strawberry Tarts: Substitute 1 package (10 ounces) frozen strawberry halves in light syrup for raspberries.

DOUBLE CHOCOLATE PUDDING PIE

*We doubled the rich chocolate flavor to double the goodness
of this frozen dessert (photo, page 61).*

Prep time: 20 minutes plus freezing

I cup cold milk

I package (4-serving size) JELL-O Chocolate Flavor Instant
    Pudding & Pie Filling

2 squares BAKER'S Semi-Sweet Chocolate, melted

2 cups thawed COOL WHIP Whipped Topping

I graham cracker crumb crust *or* baked pastry shell
    (6 ounces *or* 9 inches)

1. Pour milk into medium bowl. Add pudding mix.
Beat with wire whisk 2 minutes. Let stand 5 minutes
or until thickened.

2. Gradually mix in chocolate until smooth. Gently
stir in whipped topping. Spoon mixture into crust.

3. Freeze 4 hours or until firm. Garnish with
chocolate curls. Store leftover pie in freezer.

Makes 8 servings.

CREAMY CHOCOLATE LAYERED PIE

*It takes just minutes to mix up this rich and delicious pie. If you like, garnish with
chocolate curls or cutouts for an extra-pretty dessert (photo, pages 44–45).*

Prep time: 20 minutes plus refrigerating

4 ounces PHILADELPHIA BRAND Cream Cheese, softened

I tablespoon milk *or* half-and-half

I tablespoon sugar

I tub (12 ounces) COOL WHIP Whipped Topping, thawed,
    divided

I prepared chocolate flavor crumb crust (6 ounces)

1½ cups cold milk *or* half-and-half

2 packages (4-serving size each) JELL-O Chocolate Flavor
    Instant Pudding & Pie Filling

1. Mix cream cheese, 1 tablespoon milk and sugar
in large bowl with wire whisk until smooth. Gently
stir in 1½ cups of the whipped topping. Spread on
bottom of crust.

2. Pour 1½ cups milk into large bowl. Add
pudding mixes. Beat with wire whisk 1 minute.
(Mixture will be thick.) Gently stir in 2 cups of the
whipped topping. Spread over cream cheese layer.

3. Refrigerate 4 hours or until set. Garnish with
remaining whipped topping, if desired. Store leftover pie in refrigerator.

Makes 8 servings.

APPLE TOPPED CREAM PIE

Here's a delectable variation on the familiar apple pie—it features apple slices atop a filling of vanilla pudding and Neufchatel cheese (photo, page 64).

Prep time: 20 minutes plus refrigerating

- 2 cups cold milk
- 1 package (8 ounces) PHILADELPHIA BRAND Neufchatel Cheese, ⅓ Less Fat than Cream Cheese, softened
- 2 packages (4-serving size each) JELL-O Vanilla Flavor Instant Pudding & Pie Filling
- 1 teaspoon ground cinnamon, divided
- 1 graham cracker crumb crust (6 ounces *or* 9 inches)
- 1 can (20 ounces) sliced apples, drained, diced
  Sugar

1. Beat milk gradually into Neufchatel cheese in large bowl with wire whisk until smooth. Add pudding mixes and ½ teaspoon of the cinnamon. Beat 1 to 2 minutes. Spread evenly in crust.

2. Mix apples and remaining ½ teaspoon cinnamon in small bowl. Sweeten to taste with sugar. Spoon evenly over pudding mixture.

3. Refrigerate 4 hours or until set. Store leftover pie in refrigerator.

Makes 8 servings.

IRISH COFFEE PIE

Like a rich, flavored coffee drink poured into a pie shell, this dessert will be a winner at holiday gatherings.

Prep time: 10 minutes plus refrigerating

- 2 cups cold milk
- 1 tablespoon Irish whiskey
- 1 package (6-serving size) JELL-O Vanilla Flavor Instant Pudding & Pie Filling
- 2 teaspoons MAXWELL HOUSE Instant Coffee
- 1 baked pastry shell *or* graham cracker crumb crust (9 inches *or* 6 ounces)

1. Pour milk and whiskey into large bowl. Add pudding mix and instant coffee. Beat with wire whisk 2 minutes.

2. Pour mixture into pastry shell.

3. Refrigerate 4 hours or until set. Garnish with whipped topping and sprinkle with cinnamon or toasted coconut. Store leftover pie in refrigerator.

Makes 8 servings.

HOLIDAY POKE CAKE

Use red and green JELL-O gelatin, such as raspberry and lime flavors, to create
holiday-colored swirls through this tempting cake (photo, page 61).

Prep time: 20 minutes plus refrigerating

- 2 baked 9-inch round white cake layers, cooled
- 2 cups boiling water, divided
- 1 package (4-serving size) JELL-O Brand Gelatin, any red flavor
- 1 package (4-serving size) JELL-O Brand Lime Flavor Gelatin
- 1 tub (12 ounces) COOL WHIP Whipped Topping, thawed

1. Place cake layers, top sides up, in 2 clean 9-inch round cake pans. Pierce cake with large fork at ½-inch intervals.

2. Stir 1 cup of the boiling water into each flavor of gelatin in separate bowls 2 minutes or until completely dissolved. Carefully pour red gelatin over 1 cake layer and lime gelatin over second cake layer.

3. Refrigerate 3 hours. Dip 1 cake pan in warm water 10 seconds; unmold onto serving plate. Spread with about 1 cup of the whipped topping. Unmold second cake layer; carefully place on first layer. Frost top and sides of cake with remaining whipped topping.

4. Refrigerate at least 1 hour or until ready to serve. Decorate as desired. Store leftover cake in refrigerator.

Makes 12 servings.

SHARE THE HOLIDAYS

For a New Year's celebration, set time aside for a family awards dinner or party. Acknowledge major family events and accomplishments from the previous year, such as hitting a home run during a Little League baseball game or completing a major home-improvement chore. You can even present gag awards for funny incidents. Have a friend or family member videotape the ceremony as a record of your family history, so you can enjoy it in the years to come.

DOUBLE LAYER PUMPKIN PIE

*Light and creamy, this no-bake pie will
become a family favorite.*

Prep time: 20 minutes plus refrigerating

- 4 ounces PHILADELPHIA BRAND Cream Cheese, softened
- 1 tablespoon milk or half-and-half
- 1 tablespoon sugar
- 1½ cups thawed COOL WHIP Whipped Topping
- 1 graham cracker crumb crust (6 ounces *or* 9 inches)
- 1 cup cold milk *or* half-and-half
- 1 can (16 ounces) pumpkin
- 2 packages (4-serving size each) JELL-O Vanilla Flavor Instant Pudding & Pie Filling
- 1 teaspoon ground cinnamon
- ½ teaspoon ground ginger
- ¼ teaspoon ground cloves

1. Mix cream cheese, 1 tablespoon milk and sugar in large bowl with wire whisk until smooth. Gently stir in whipped topping. Spread on bottom of crust.

2. Pour 1 cup milk into large bowl. Add pumpkin, pudding mixes and spices. Beat with wire whisk 2 minutes. (Mixture will be thick.) Spread over cream cheese layer.

3. Refrigerate 4 hours or until set. Garnish with additional whipped topping and chocolate-dipped pecan halves. Store leftover pie in refrigerator.

Makes 8 servings.

SHARE THE HOLIDAYS

After the holidays, have an "undecorating" party. "Plundering the tree," a Scandinavian tradition, turns an after-holiday chore into a celebration. Here's how it works: Each participating family removes the ornaments from its tree, placing a few of the ornaments on a table with some refreshments. The families then visit each others' homes and take one ornament from each family to use on their tree the following year. The result is an extra chance to enjoy holiday cheer with friends and share memories that will be represented by the ornaments in the years to come.

Double Layer Pumpkin Pie

HEAVENLY CHOCOLATE CAKE

*Made with MIRACLE WHIP Salad Dressing, this moist cake deserves
its name. A rich chocolate-cream cheese frosting enriches the
out-of-this-world concoction even more (photos, right and cover).*

Prep time: 10 minutes
Baking time: 35 minutes plus cooling

CAKE:

- 1 package (2-layer size) chocolate cake mix (*not* variety with pudding)
- ½ cup unsweetened cocoa
- 3 eggs
- 1⅓ cups water
- 1 cup MIRACLE WHIP Salad Dressing

FROSTING:

- 1 package (8 ounces) PHILADELPHIA BRAND Cream Cheese, softened
- 2 tablespoons milk
- 1 teaspoon vanilla
- 5 cups sifted powdered sugar
- ½ cup unsweetened cocoa

1. *To prepare cake:* Heat oven to 350°F. Grease and flour 2 (9-inch) round cake pans. Line bottom of pans with wax paper.

2. Stir cake mix and cocoa in large mixing bowl; add remaining cake ingredients. Beat with electric mixer on low speed 30 seconds, scraping bowl frequently. Beat with electric mixer on medium speed 2 minutes. Pour batter into prepared pans.

3. Bake 30 to 35 minutes or until toothpick inserted in center comes out clean. Cool 10 minutes; remove from pans. Immediately remove wax paper. Cool completely on wire racks.

4. *To prepare frosting:* Beat cream cheese, milk and vanilla with electric mixer on medium speed until well blended. Mix powdered sugar and cocoa in another bowl. Gradually add to cream cheese mixture, beating well after each addition. Fill and frost cake layers.

Makes 12 servings.

For sheet cake: Substitute greased and floured 13x9-inch baking pan for 9-inch round cake pans. Bake 35 to 40 minutes or until toothpick inserted in center comes out clean. Cool on wire rack. Do not remove cake from pan to frost. Frost as desired.

For triple-layer cake: Heat oven to 350°F. Grease and flour 3 (9-inch) round cake pans. Line bottom of pans with wax paper. Prepare cake batter as directed. Divide batter between 3 prepared pans. Bake 20 to 23 minutes or until toothpick inserted in center comes out clean.

•Cool 10 minutes; remove from pans. Immediately remove wax paper. Cool completely on wire racks. Fill and frost as desired.

CAPE COD BLUEBERRY CAKE

*Wake up to the great taste of fresh blueberries
with this quick-to-fix cake.*

Prep time: 20 minutes

Baking time: 40 minutes

1¾ cups flour

1 teaspoon baking soda

¾ teaspoon CALUMET Baking Powder

½ teaspoon salt

½ teaspoon ground cinnamon

¼ teaspoon ground nutmeg

½ cup (1 stick) PARKAY Spread Sticks

¾ cup sugar

1 egg

1 cup hot water

¼ cup light corn syrup

2 cups POST BLUEBERRY MORNING Cereal

1. Heat oven to 350°F.

2. Mix flour, baking soda, baking powder, salt, cinnamon and nutmeg in medium bowl. Beat PARKAY and sugar in large bowl with electric mixer on medium speed until light and fluffy. Beat in egg. Gradually beat in water and corn syrup. Add flour mixture, beating until smooth. Stir in cereal. Pour into greased and floured 9-inch square pan.

3. Bake 40 minutes or until toothpick inserted in center comes out clean. Serve warm. Sprinkle with powdered sugar.

Makes 12 servings.

Flavored Coffees

*For a relaxing after-dinner treat or a warm beverage on a
chilly evening, try one of these luscious dessert coffees
(photos, pages 44–45).*

Brandied Coffee:
Stir 1 ounce brandy into 6 ounces hot brewed
YUBAN *or* MAXWELL HOUSE Coffee in a glass mug.
Garnish with COOL WHIP Whipped Topping and
grated BAKER'S Semi-Sweet Chocolate.

French Coffee:
Pour 1 ounce brandy and ½ ounce orange-flavored
liqueur into a mug; fill with 6 ounces hot brewed
YUBAN *or* MAXWELL HOUSE Coffee. Add cream to
taste. Garnish with COOL WHIP Whipped Topping
and orange wedge.

Snuggler:
Add 1 envelope instant cocoa and 1½ ounces
brandy to 6 ounces hot brewed YUBAN *or*
MAXWELL HOUSE Coffee; stir to dissolve instant
cocoa. Garnish with COOL WHIP Whipped Topping
and holiday sprinkles.

Share the Holidays

Celebrate the holiday traditions of neighbors and friends by hosting a potluck
party where each family shares a food or tradition from its heritage. One guest
might bring a traditional Hanukkah food such as latkes—potato pancakes, while
another might explain the seven principles of the African Kwanzaa. To create a
special remembrance of this celebration, ask each guest to write down the shared
recipe or tradition. Then, after the holidays are over, photocopy the materials,
compile them with a few photographs from the party into books, and distribute a
book to each guest.

PHILLY 3-STEP™ CARAMEL PECAN CHEESECAKE

It's as easy as one, two, three to prepare this luscious praline cheesecake.

Prep time: 10 minutes
Baking time: 40 minutes

 2 packages (8 ounces each) **PHILADELPHIA BRAND** Cream Cheese, softened
 ½ cup sugar
 ½ teaspoon vanilla
 2 eggs
 20 KRAFT Caramels
 2 tablespoons milk
 ½ cup chopped pecans
 1 ready-to-use graham cracker crumb crust
   (**6** ounces *or* **9** inches)

1. MIX cream cheese, sugar and vanilla with electric mixer on medium speed until well blended. Add eggs; mix until blended.

2. MELT caramels with milk in saucepan on low heat, stirring frequently until smooth. Stir in pecans. Spread on bottom of crust. Pour cream cheese batter over caramel mixture.

3. BAKE at 350°F for 40 minutes or until center is almost set. Cool. Refrigerate 3 hours or overnight. Garnish with pecan halves dipped in melted chocolate and chocolate whipped cream.

Makes 8 servings.

PHILLY 3-STEP™ PUMPKIN CHEESECAKE

For a new twist to the traditional pumpkin pie try this incredible pumpkin cheesecake (photo, pages 44–45).

Prep time: 10 minutes
Baking time: 40 minutes

 2 packages (8 ounces each) **PHILADELPHIA BRAND** Cream Cheese, softened
 ½ cup sugar
 ½ cup canned pumpkin
 ½ teaspoon ground cinnamon
 ½ teaspoon vanilla
   Dash *each* ground cloves and nutmeg
 2 eggs
 1 ready-to-use graham cracker crumb crust
   (**6** ounces *or* **9** inches)

1. MIX cream cheese, sugar, pumpkin, cinnamon, vanilla, cloves and nutmeg with electric mixer on medium speed until well blended. Add eggs; mix until blended.

2. POUR into crust.

3. BAKE at 350°F for 40 minutes or until center is almost set. Cool. Refrigerate 3 hours or overnight. Garnish with COOL WHIP Whipped Topping.

Makes 8 servings.

ONE BOWL® Brownies (recipe, page 59)
PHILLY 3-STEP™ Caramel Pecan Cheesecake

SECRETS FOR SUCCESSFUL DESSERTS

Here are some quick tips from the Kraft Creative Kitchens for making the best use of the Family of Fine Food Products from Kraft Foods.

BAKER'S CHOCOLATE

- Store the chocolate in a cool, dry place. It should be below 75°F, if possible, but not in the refrigerator.
- Use the type of chocolate called for in a recipe. As a rule, semi-sweet chocolate and unsweetened chocolate are not interchangeable in recipes.
- Use of a microwave for melting chocolate is strongly recommended. Chocolate scorches easily on top of the stove so use very low heat and a heavy saucepan when using this method.

  Microwave method: Heat 1 unwrapped square of BAKER'S Semi-Sweet or Unsweetened Chocolate or 1 unwrapped 4-ounce bar of BAKER'S GERMAN'S Sweet Chocolate, broken in half, in microwavable bowl on HIGH 1 to 2 minutes or until almost melted, stirring halfway through heating time. The chocolate pieces will retain some of their original shape. Remove from oven. Stir until chocolate is completely melted. Add 10 seconds for each additional square.

  Stovetop method: Place unwrapped chocolate in heavy saucepan on very low heat; stir constantly until just melted.

COOL WHIP WHIPPED TOPPING

- COOL WHIP Non-Dairy Extra Creamy and COOL WHIP LITE Whipped Toppings usually can be used interchangeably in recipes. If COOL WHIP LITE is used with gelatin or higher acid fruits, the recipe may not set as firmly. Make sure to use the cup measurement specified in the recipe.

JELL-O INSTANT PUDDING & PIE FILLING

- Always use cold milk. Beat pudding mix slowly, not vigorously.

PHILADELPHIA BRAND CREAM CHEESE

- When a recipe calls for softened PHILADELPHIA BRAND Cream Cheese or PHILADELPHIA BRAND Neufchatel Cheese, ⅓ Less Fat than Cream Cheese, soften it in microwave on HIGH 15 to 20 seconds.

PUMPKIN SNACK BARS

Freeze any leftovers so you'll always have goodies on hand.

Prep time: 20 minutes
Baking time: 20 minutes plus cooling

CAKE:

- 1 package (2-layer size) spice cake mix
- 1 can (16 ounces) pumpkin
- ¾ cup MIRACLE WHIP *or* MIRACLE WHIP LIGHT Dressing
- 3 eggs

FROSTING:

- 3½ cups powdered sugar
- ½ cup (1 stick) PARKAY Spread Sticks, softened
- 2 tablespoons milk
- 1 teaspoon vanilla

1. *To prepare cake:* Heat oven to 350°F.

2. Beat cake mix, pumpkin, dressing and eggs with electric mixer on medium speed until well blended. Pour into greased 15x10x1-inch baking pan.

3. Bake 18 to 20 minutes or until toothpick inserted in center comes out clean. Cool completely on wire rack.

4. *To prepare frosting:* Beat all ingredients with electric mixer on low speed until moistened. Beat on high speed until light and fluffy. Spread over cake. Cut into bars. Garnish with shredded orange peel.

Makes about 3 dozen.

ONE BOWL® BROWNIES

So simple, so good (photos, page 56 and cover).

Prep time: 20 minutes
Microwave cooking time: 2 minutes
Baking time: 30 minutes plus cooling

- 4 squares BAKER'S Unsweetened Chocolate
- ¾ cup (1½ sticks) margarine *or* butter
- 2 cups sugar
- 3 eggs
- 1 teaspoon vanilla
- 1 cup flour
- 1 cup coarsely chopped nuts (optional)

1. Heat oven to 350°F (325°F for glass baking dish).

2. Microwave chocolate and margarine in microwavable bowl on HIGH 2 minutes or until margarine is melted. Stir until chocolate is completely melted.

3. Stir sugar into chocolate until blended. Mix in eggs and vanilla. Stir in flour and nuts. Spread in greased foil-lined 13x9-inch baking pan.

4. Bake 30 minutes or until toothpick inserted in center comes out with fudgy crumbs. *Do not overbake.* Cool in pan. Cut into squares or into decorative shapes with cookie cutters and sprinkle with powdered sugar.

Makes 2 dozen.

EASY CHOCOLATE HOLIDAY DESSERT

A sensationally rich dessert of cake, chocolate and toffee.

Prep time: 20 minutes plus refrigerating

- 3 cups cold milk
- 2 packages (4-serving size each) JELL-O Chocolate Flavor Instant Pudding & Pie Filling
- 1 tub (8 ounces) COOL WHIP Whipped Topping, thawed, divided
- 1 package (12 ounces) marble pound cake, cut into ½-inch cubes
- ⅓ cup chocolate-flavored syrup
- 4 bars (1.4 ounces each) chocolate-covered English toffee, chopped

1. Pour milk into large bowl. Add pudding mixes. Beat with wire whisk 1 minute. Let stand 5 minutes. Gently stir in 2 cups of the whipped topping.

2. Arrange ½ of the cake cubes in 3½-quart serving bowl. Drizzle with ½ of the chocolate-flavored syrup. Layer with ½ of the chopped toffee bars and ½ of the pudding mixture. Repeat layers.

3. Refrigerate 1 hour or until ready to serve. Top with remaining whipped topping. Garnish with fresh mint leaves and raspberries. Store leftover dessert in refrigerator.

Makes 12 servings.

PEPPERMINT PARFAITS

For a graceful garnish, hang a candy cane from each glass (photo, page 64).

Prep time: 20 minutes plus refrigerating

- 1 cup boiling water
- 1 package (4-serving size) JELL-O Brand Raspberry *or* Lime Flavor Gelatin
- ¾ cup cold water
- 2 teaspoons white crème de menthe (optional)
- 1 cup thawed COOL WHIP Whipped Topping, divided

1. Stir boiling water into gelatin in medium bowl 2 minutes or until completely dissolved. Stir in cold water and crème de menthe. Reserve 1 cup of the mixture; let stand at room temperature. Refrigerate remaining gelatin 45 minutes or until slightly thickened (consistency of unbeaten egg whites).

2. Stir ½ cup of the whipped topping into slightly thickened gelatin with wire whisk until smooth and creamy. Pour mixture into 4 parfait glasses. Refrigerate 1½ hours or until set but not firm (should stick to finger when touched). Pour reserved gelatin evenly over creamy layers.

3. Refrigerate 3 hours or until firm. Garnish each parfait with remaining whipped topping and peppermint candy just before serving, if desired.

Makes 4 servings.

Clockwise from top left: Easy Chocolate Holiday Dessert, Holiday Poke Cake (recipe, page 49), Jigglers® Holiday Time Gelatin (recipe, page 65), Double Chocolate Pudding Pie (recipe, page 47)

Pumpkin Rice Pudding

This unique pudding tastes just like pumpkin pie without a crust.
Dress up each serving with slices of kumquats, orange peel twists or a
dollop of COOL WHIP Whipped Topping.

Prep time: 15 minutes
Baking time: 50 minutes

  4 cups milk
  I can (16 ounces) pumpkin
  I cup MINUTE Original Rice, uncooked
¾ cup sugar
  I teaspoon ground cinnamon
½ teaspoon *each* ground ginger and salt
¼ teaspoon ground cloves
  2 eggs
½ teaspoon vanilla

1. Heat oven to 375°F.

2. Bring milk, pumpkin, rice, sugar, cinnamon, ginger, salt and cloves to boil in large saucepan, stirring constantly. Reduce heat to low; simmer 5 minutes, stirring occasionally. Remove from heat.

3. Beat eggs and vanilla in large bowl. Slowly stir in hot pumpkin mixture, blending well after each addition. Pour into greased 2-quart casserole.

4. Bake 45 to 50 minutes or until set. Cool slightly. Serve warm or refrigerate until ready to serve.

Makes 14 servings.

CHOCOLATE CANDY BAR DESSERT

With a cookie crust and candy-bar filling, this will be a bit
with choco-holics and children of all ages.

Prep time: 20 minutes plus refrigerating

2 cups chocolate wafer cookie crumbs
½ cup sugar, divided
½ cup (1 stick) PARKAY Spread Sticks, melted
1 package (8 ounces) PHILADELPHIA BRAND Cream Cheese,
  softened
1 tub (12 ounces) COOL WHIP Whipped Topping, thawed,
  divided
1 cup chopped chocolate-covered candy bars
3 cups cold milk
2 packages (4-serving size each) JELL-O Chocolate Flavor
  Instant Pudding & Pie Filling

1. Mix cookie crumbs, ¼ cup of the sugar and
PARKAY in 13x9-inch pan. Press firmly onto bottom
of pan. Refrigerate 10 minutes.

2. Mix cream cheese and remaining ¼ cup sugar
in medium bowl with wire whisk until smooth.
Gently stir in ½ of the whipped topping. Spread
evenly over crust. Sprinkle chopped candy bars
over cream cheese layer.

3. Pour milk into large bowl. Add pudding mixes.
Beat with wire whisk 1 minute. Pour over chopped
candy bar layer. Let stand 5 minutes or until
thickened. Spread remaining whipped topping over
pudding layer.

4. Refrigerate 2 hours or until set. Garnish with
additional chopped candy bars. Cut into squares.
Store leftover dessert in refrigerator.

Makes 15 to 18 servings.

CREAMY HOLIDAY LEMON CUPS

It's like eating eggnog with a spoon.

Prep time: 15 minutes plus refrigerating

- 2 cups boiling water
- 1 package (8-serving size) *or* 2 packages (4-serving size each) JELL-O Brand Lemon Flavor Gelatin
- ½ cup cold water
- 1½ cups cold milk
- 1 package (4-serving size) JELL-O Vanilla Flavor Instant Pudding & Pie Filling
- 2 teaspoons rum extract
- ½ teaspoon ground nutmeg
- 2 cups thawed COOL WHIP Whipped Topping

1. Stir boiling water into gelatin in large bowl 2 minutes or until completely dissolved. Stir in cold water. Cool to room temperature.

2. Pour milk into another bowl. Add pudding mix. Beat with wire whisk 30 seconds. Immediately stir into cooled gelatin until smooth. Stir in rum extract and nutmeg. Refrigerate about 1¼ hours or until slightly thickened.

3. Stir in whipped topping with wire whisk until smooth and creamy. Pour into 10 individual dessert dishes or drinking mugs.

4. Refrigerate 4 hours or until firm. Garnish with additional whipped topping and sprinkle with additional ground nutmeg just before serving.

Makes 10 servings.

JIGGLERS® HOLIDAY TIME GELATIN

For giggles of delight, make JELL-O Gelatin reindeer or Santas (photo, page 61).

Prep time: 10 minutes plus refrigerating

- 2½ cups boiling water *or* boiling fruit juice *(Do not add cold water or cold juice.)*
- 2 packages (8-serving size each) *or* 4 packages (4-serving size each) JELL-O Brand Gelatin *or* JELL-O Brand Sugar Free Low Calorie Gelatin Dessert, any flavor

1. Stir boiling water into gelatin in large bowl 3 minutes or until completely dissolved. Pour into 13x9-inch pan.

2. Refrigerate at least 3 hours or until firm (does not stick to finger when touched).

3. Dip bottom of pan in warm water about 15 seconds. Cut into decorative shapes with cookie cutters all the way through gelatin or cut into 1-inch squares. Lift from pan.

Makes about 24 pieces.

Note: If you like, recipe can be halved. Substitute 8- or 9-inch square pan for 13x9-inch pan.

Clockwise from top left: Peppermint Parfaits (recipe, page 60), Apple Topped Cream Pie (recipe, page 48), Creamy Holiday Lemon Cups

GIFTS IN GOOD TASTE

From the heart and hearth, these homemade presents capture the spirit of the holiday season. Each tastefully selected recipe— for everything from candies and cookies to sweet breads—includes a simple, yet clever, gift-giving idea that tells the recipients they're *special*.

Clockwise from top right:
Marble Bark (recipe, page 68),
Chocolate Cherry Thumbprint Cookies
(recipe, page 78),
Gift-Giving Cereal Bread
(recipe, page 80)

FANTASY FUDGE

For a pretty presentation, wrap each piece of fudge in colorful foil, then place them in a striking holiday tin or box (photo, above).

Prep time: 10 minutes plus cooling
Cooking time: 15 minutes

- ¾ cup (1½ sticks) **PARKAY** Spread Sticks
- 3 cups sugar
- 1 can (5 ounces) evaporated milk* (⅔ cup)
- 1 package (12 ounces) **BAKER'S** Semi-Sweet Real Chocolate Chips
- 1 jar (7 ounces) **KRAFT** Marshmallow Creme
- 1 cup chopped nuts (optional)
- 1 teaspoon vanilla

1. Lightly grease 13x9-inch or 9-inch square pan.

2. Mix PARKAY, sugar and milk in heavy 2½- to 3- quart saucepan; bring to full rolling boil on medium heat, stirring constantly.

3. Continue boiling 5 minutes on medium heat or until candy thermometer reaches 234°F, stirring constantly to prevent scorching. Remove from heat.

4. Gradually stir in chips until melted. Add remaining ingredients; mix well.

5. Pour into prepared pan. Cool at room temperature; cut into squares.

Makes about 3 pounds.

*Do not substitute sweetened condensed milk for evaporated milk.

MARBLE BARK

Add a splash of color to your gift by lining your container with colored tissue paper or cellophane (photo, pages 66–67).

Prep time: 20 minutes plus refrigerating
Microwave cooking time: 2 minutes

- 6 squares **BAKER'S** Semi-Sweet Chocolate
- 1 package (6 squares) **BAKER'S** Premium White Chocolate
- 1 cup toasted chopped nuts *or* toasted **BAKER'S** ANGEL FLAKE Coconut, divided

1. Microwave semi-sweet and white chocolates in separate microwavable bowls on HIGH 2 minutes or until chocolates are almost melted, stirring halfway through heating time. Stir until chocolates are completely melted.

2. Stir ½ cup of the nuts into each bowl. Alternately spoon melted chocolates onto wax paper-lined cookie sheet or tray. Swirl chocolates with knife several times for marble effect.

3. Refrigerate 1 hour or until firm. Break into pieces.

Makes about 1 pound.

Festive Nut Bark: Prepare recipe as directed, omitting Semi-Sweet Chocolate. Use 2 packages (6 squares each) BAKER'S Premium White Chocolate. Stir in ½ cup toasted chopped almonds *or* pistachios.

ONE BOWL® CHOCOLATE FUDGE

For an even more thoughtful gift, make several kinds of fudge using our speedy variations so you can give an assortment to friends.

Prep time: 20 minutes plus refrigerating
Microwave cooking time: 2 minutes

- 2 packages (8 squares each) BAKER'S Semi-Sweet Chocolate
- 1 can (14 ounces) sweetened condensed milk
- 2 teaspoons vanilla
- 1 cup chopped nuts *or* toasted BAKER'S ANGEL FLAKE Coconut (optional)

1. Microwave chocolate and milk in microwavable bowl on HIGH 2 minutes or until chocolate is almost melted, stirring halfway through heating time. Stir until chocolate is completely melted.

2. Stir in vanilla and nuts. Spread in foil-lined 8-inch square pan.

3. Refrigerate 2 hours or until firm. Cut into squares.

Makes about 4 dozen.

Peanut Butter Swirl Fudge: Prepare Fudge as directed, omitting nuts. Drop ½ cup peanut butter by teaspoonfuls on top of fudge. Swirl with knife several times for marble effect.

Cherry White Fudge: Prepare Fudge as directed, using 1 cup toasted chopped almonds for nuts. Spread in pan. Before refrigerating fudge, melt 1 package (6 squares) BAKER'S Premium White Chocolate as directed on package. Stir in ½ cup sweetened condensed milk and ½ cup dried cherries. Spread over Fudge in pan.

Note: Fudge refrigerated longer than 2 hours may be too firm to cut. Let stand at room temperature about 30 minutes to make cutting easier.

CRISPY MARSHMALLOW TREE

Colorful candies create instant "ornaments" on this edible tree. Make several trees this holiday season to please your neighbors and friends.

Prep time: 20 minutes
Microwave cooking time: 2 minutes
and 15 seconds plus cooling OR
Stovetop cooking time: 5 minutes
plus cooling

- 3 tablespoons PARKAY Spread Sticks
- 1 package (10½ ounces) KRAFT Miniature Marshmallows (6 cups)
- ½ teaspoon green food coloring (optional)
- 6 cups crisp rice cereal
- ¾ cup candy-coated milk chocolate candies, divided
  Chewy candies, cut into star shapes
  Red licorice
  Decorating icing

1. Grease 13x9-inch pan.

2. Microwave PARKAY in large microwavable bowl on HIGH 45 seconds or until melted. Add marshmallows; toss to coat with PARKAY. Microwave on HIGH 1½ minutes or until smooth when stirred, stirring after 45 seconds. Stir in food coloring.

3. Immediately add cereal and ½ cup of the chocolate candies; mix lightly until well coated. Using greased spatula or wax paper, press into prepared pan. Cool.

4. Cut 1 (2-inch-wide) piece vertically across end of pan as shown in Diagram 1; divide into 4 equal pieces (A, B, C and D). Place pieces A and B at base to form the trunk of the tree. Decorate pieces C and D with decorating icing as presents or stack them on top of pieces A and B for larger tree trunk. Cut remaining mixture in pan into 1 large triangle

and 2 smaller triangle pieces (E, F and G) as shown in Diagram 1. Arrange pieces E and F on tray as shown in Diagram 2. Place piece G on top; garnish with remaining ¼ cup chocolate candies, chewy candies, licorice and decorating icing.

Makes 24 servings.

To cook on stove: Melt PARKAY in 3-quart saucepan on low heat.

• Add marshmallows; stir until marshmallows are melted and mixture is smooth. Remove from heat. Stir in food coloring.

• Continue as directed.

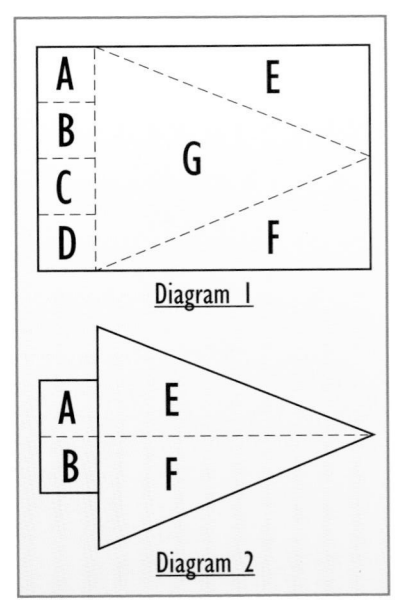

Diagram 1

Diagram 2

CHOCOLATE PIZZA

*Ideal for coworkers or as Secret Santa gifts, these pizzas can
be made in a variety of sizes.*

Prep time: 15 minutes plus refrigerating
Microwave cooking time: 6 minutes OR
Stovetop cooking time: 10 minutes

- 1 package (12 ounces) BAKER'S Semi-Sweet Real Chocolate Chips
- 1 pound white almond bark, divided
- 2 cups KRAFT Miniature Marshmallows
- 1 cup crisp rice cereal
- 1 cup peanuts
- 1 jar (6 ounces) red maraschino cherries, drained, cut in half
- 3 tablespoons green maraschino cherries, drained, quartered
- 1/3 cup BAKER'S ANGEL FLAKE Coconut
- 1 teaspoon oil

1. Microwave chips and 14 ounces of the almond bark in 2-quart microwavable bowl on HIGH 2 minutes; stir. Continue microwaving 1 to 2 minutes or until smooth when stirred, stirring every 30 seconds.

2. Stir in marshmallows, cereal and peanuts. Pour onto greased 12-inch pizza pan. Top with cherries; sprinkle with coconut.

3. Microwave remaining 2 ounces almond bark and oil in 1-cup glass measuring cup 1 minute; stir. Continue microwaving 30 seconds to 1 minute or until smooth when stirred, stirring every 15 seconds. Drizzle over coconut.

4. Refrigerate until firm. Store at room temperature.

Makes 10 to 12 servings.

To cook on stove: Melt chips and 14 ounces of the almond bark in large saucepan on low heat, stirring until smooth. Remove from heat.

- Stir in marshmallows, cereal and peanuts. Pour onto greased 12-inch pizza pan. Top with cherries; sprinkle with coconut.

- Melt remaining 2 ounces almond bark with oil on low heat, stirring until smooth. Drizzle over coconut.

- Refrigerate until firm. Store at room temperature.

Individual Chocolate Pizzas: Spoon chocolate mixture onto greased cookie sheet, forming 3 (7-inch) or 4 (6-inch) circles with back of wooden spoon. Continue as directed.

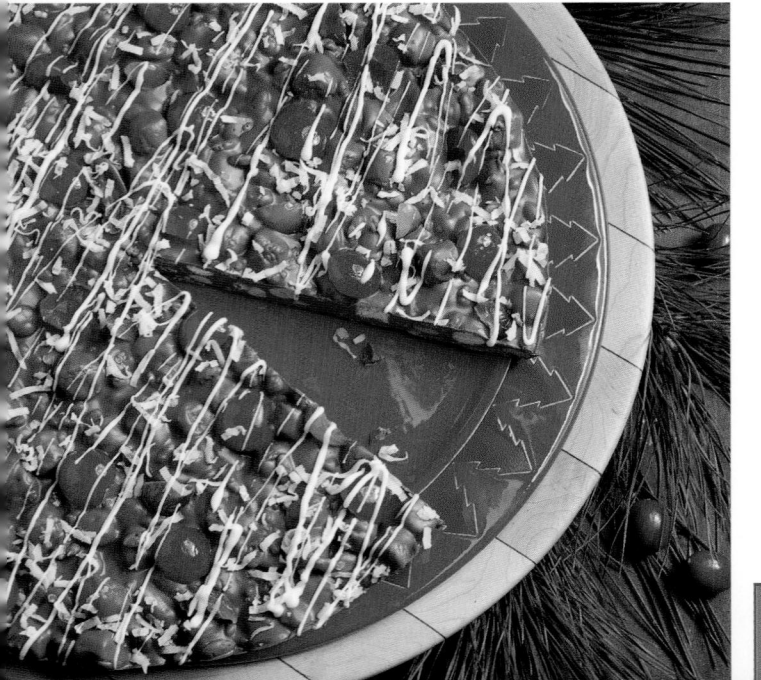

HOLIDAY PEPPERMINT CANDIES

Perfect for a holiday bazaar or wrapped as party favors, these candies are especially pretty when you use cookie stamps to give them a decorative design.

Prep time: 30 minutes plus refrigerating

- 4 ounces PHILADELPHIA BRAND Cream Cheese, softened
- 1 tablespoon PARKAY Spread Sticks
- 1 tablespoon light corn syrup
- ¼ teaspoon peppermint extract *or* a few drops peppermint oil
- 4 cups powdered sugar
  Green and red food coloring
  Sifted powdered sugar
  Green, red and white decorating icing (optional)

1. Beat cream cheese, PARKAY, corn syrup and extract in large bowl with electric mixer on medium speed until well blended. Gradually add 4 cups sugar; mix well.

2. Divide mixture into thirds. Knead a few drops green food coloring into first third; repeat with red food coloring and second third. Wrap each third in plastic wrap.

3. Working with 1 color mixture at a time, shape into ¾-inch balls. Place on wax paper-lined cookie sheet. Flatten each ball with bottom of glass that has been lightly dipped in sifted powdered sugar.

4. Repeat with remaining mixtures. Decorate with icing. Store candies in refrigerator.

Makes 5 dozen.

CHEWY CARAMEL BARS

Choose from a variety of containers, such as decorative tins, unusual plates and brightly colored sand pails, to create a clever gift (photo, page 74).

Prep time: 20 minutes plus refrigerating
Microwave cooking time: 2 minutes

- 8 cups POST GOLDEN CRISP Sweetened Puffed Wheat Cereal
- 1 cup peanuts
- 1 package (14 ounces) KRAFT Caramels
- 2 tablespoons water

1. Mix cereal and peanuts in large bowl.

2. Microwave caramels and water in microwavable bowl on HIGH 2 minutes or until caramels are melted, stirring every minute. Pour immediately over cereal mixture. Mix lightly until well coated.

3. With lightly greased hands, press firmly into greased 13x9-inch pan. Refrigerate until firm. Cut into bars. Store in tightly covered container.

Makes 32.

CEREAL PEANUT BUTTER CUPS

*For gift giving, wrap these cups individually in colorful
plastic wrap, then tie each with a bright red ribbon.*

Prep time: 20 minutes plus refrigerating

⅓ cup peanut butter

¼ cup (½ stick) PARKAY Spread Sticks

3 cups KRAFT Miniature Marshmallows

3 cups POST Cocoa PEBBLES Cereal

¾ cup powdered sugar

1 tablespoon milk

1. Melt peanut butter and PARKAY in medium saucepan on low heat. Add marshmallows; stir until melted. Remove from heat.

2. Add cereal; mix to coat well. Spoon ¼ cup of the mixture into each of 12 paper-lined muffin cups. Refrigerate about 1 hour or until firm.

3. Mix sugar and milk. Drizzle over cereal mixture.

Makes 12.

KRIS KRINGLE COOKIES

*Filled with fruit and nuts, these cookies pack pleasure in every bite.
Try the variation for assorted gift giving.*

Prep time: 15 minutes
Baking time per cookie sheet: 12 minutes plus cooling

½ cup (1 stick) margarine *or* butter, softened

½ cup granulated sugar

¼ cup firmly packed brown sugar

1 egg

½ teaspoon vanilla

1 cup flour

1 teaspoon baking soda

¼ teaspoon salt

6 squares BAKER'S Semi-Sweet Chocolate, chopped*

2 cups toasted chopped walnuts*

1½ cups dried fruit*

1. Heat oven to 375°F.

2. Beat margarine and sugars in large bowl with electric mixer on medium speed until light and fluffy. Beat in egg and vanilla. Mix in flour, baking soda and salt. Stir in chocolate, walnuts and dried fruit. Drop by rounded tablespoonfuls, 1½ inches apart, onto ungreased cookie sheets.

3. Bake 12 minutes or until golden brown. Cool 3 minutes; remove from cookie sheets. Cool completely on wire racks. Store in tightly covered container.

Makes about 3 dozen.

*White & Bright Cookies: Or use BAKER'S Premium White Chocolate, almonds and chopped apricots.

Chewy Caramel Bars (recipe, page 73)
Cereal Peanut Butter Cups

PHILLY® CREAM CHEESE COOKIES

One basic dough lends itself to four festive cookies.

Prep time: 20 minutes plus refrigerating
Baking time per cookie sheet: 12 to 20 minutes, depending on variation, plus cooling

- 1 package (8 ounces) PHILADELPHIA BRAND Cream Cheese, softened
- ¾ cup butter
- 1 cup powdered sugar
- 2¼ cups flour
- ½ teaspoon baking soda

1. Beat cream cheese, butter and sugar with electric mixer on medium speed until well blended.

2. Add flour and baking soda; mix well. Use dough in 1 of the following variations. Makes 3 cups dough.

Chocolate Mint Cutouts: Add ¼ teaspoon mint extract and a few drops green food coloring to 1½ cups cookie dough; mix well. Refrigerate 30 minutes.
- Heat oven to 325°F. On lightly floured surface, roll dough to ⅛-inch thickness; cut with assorted 3-inch cookie cutters. Place on ungreased cookie sheet. Bake 10 to 12 minutes or until edges begin to brown. Cool on wire rack.
- Melt ¼ cup mint-flavored semi-sweet chocolate chips on low heat, stirring until smooth. Drizzle over cookies.

Makes about 3 dozen.

Snowmen: Add ¼ teaspoon vanilla to 1½ cups cookie dough; mix well. Refrigerate 30 minutes.

- For each snowman, shape dough into 2 small balls, one slightly larger than the other. Place balls, overlapping slightly, on ungreased cookie sheet; flatten with bottom of glass. Bake 18 to 20 minutes or until light golden brown. Cool on wire rack.
- Sprinkle each snowman with sifted powdered sugar. Decorate with icing as desired. Cut miniature peanut butter cups in half for hats.

Makes about 2 dozen.

Choco-Orange Slices: Add 1½ teaspoons grated orange peel to 1½ cups cookie dough; mix well. Shape into 8x1½-inch log. Refrigerate 30 minutes.
- Heat oven to 325°F. Cut log into ¼-inch slices. Place on ungreased cookie sheet. Bake 15 to 18 minutes or until edges begin to brown. Cool on wire rack.
- Melt ⅓ cup BAKER'S Semi-Sweet Real Chocolate Chips with 1 tablespoon orange juice and 1 tablespoon orange-flavored liqueur on low heat, stirring until smooth. Dip cookies into chocolate mixture.

Makes about 2½ dozen.

Preserve Thumbprints: Add ½ cup chopped pecans and ½ teaspoon vanilla to 1½ cups cookie dough; mix well. Refrigerate 30 minutes.
- Heat oven to 325°F. Shape dough into 1-inch balls. Place on ungreased cookie sheet. Indent centers; fill each with 1 teaspoon KRAFT Preserves. Bake 14 to 16 minutes or until light golden brown. Cool on wire rack.

Makes about 3½ dozen.

PHILLY® Cream Cheese Cookies (counterclockwise from top left: Preserve Thumbprints, Chocolate Mint Cutouts, Snowmen, Choco-Orange Slices)

SNOWFLAKE MACAROONS

For a candylike version, try our trouble-free chocolate variation.

Prep time: 15 minutes
Baking time per cookie sheet: 20 minutes plus cooling

- 1 package (7 ounces) BAKER'S ANGEL FLAKE Coconut (2⅔ cups)
- ⅔ cup sugar
- 6 tablespoons flour
- ¼ teaspoon salt
- 4 egg whites
- 1 teaspoon almond extract

1. Heat oven to 325°F.

2. Mix coconut, sugar, flour and salt in bowl. Stir in egg whites and extract until blended. Drop by teaspoonfuls onto lightly greased and floured cookie sheets.

3. Bake 20 minutes or until edges are golden brown. Immediately remove from cookie sheets. Cool on wire racks.

Makes 3 dozen.

Chocolate Macaroons: Stir in 2 squares melted BAKER'S Semi-Sweet Chocolate with egg whites.

CHOCOLATE CHERRY THUMBPRINT COOKIES

Perfect for a cookie exchange, this appetizing recipe makes a large batch (photos, pages 66–67 and on cover).

Prep time: 20 minutes plus refrigerating
Baking time per cookie sheet: 15 minutes plus cooling

- 1 cup (2 sticks) margarine *or* butter, softened
- ¼ teaspoon salt
- 1 cup powdered sugar
- 1 teaspoon vanilla
- 1¾ cups flour
- 1 cup finely chopped nuts
- 2 jars (8 ounces each) maraschino cherries, well drained *or* 2 cups whole candied cherries
- 4 squares BAKER'S Semi-Sweet Chocolate, melted

1. Beat margarine and salt in large bowl with electric mixer on medium speed until light and fluffy.

Gradually beat in sugar and vanilla. Mix in flour and nuts. Refrigerate dough 1 hour.

2. Heat oven to 350°F. Roll dough into ¾-inch balls. Place 1½ inches apart on ungreased cookie sheets.

3. Bake 5 minutes. Remove from oven; make depression in center of each cookie with thumb or spoon. Bake 10 minutes or until lightly browned. Cool 3 minutes; remove from cookie sheets. Cool completely on wire racks.

4. Place cherry in center of each cookie. Drizzle with melted chocolate. Let stand at room temperature until chocolate is firm.

Makes about 4 dozen.

Snowflake Macaroons
Chocolate Macaroons

PARMESAN BREADSTICK CANDY CANES

Kids will love to help you shape these candy canes. If you like, add a bit of parsley or dill to the cheese coating for extra flavor and a holiday hue.

Prep time: 10 minutes
Baking time: 18 minutes

1 can (11 ounces) refrigerated soft breadsticks
3 tablespoons PARKAY Spread Sticks, melted
½ cup (2 ounces) KRAFT 100% Grated Parmesan Cheese

1. Heat oven to 350°F.

2. Separate dough; cut each piece in half to make 16 breadsticks. Dip in PARKAY; coat with cheese. Twist and shape into candy cane shapes on ungreased cookie sheet.

3. Bake 14 to 18 minutes or until golden brown.

Makes 16.

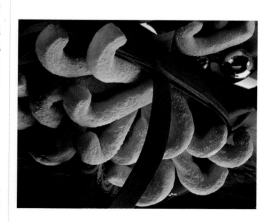

GIFT-GIVING CEREAL BREAD

Say "good morning" with a loaf of this bread, an assortment of small jams and jellies, plus a few packages of instant cocoa mix or flavored coffees (photo, pages 66–67).

Prep time: 20 minutes
Baking time: 65 minutes plus cooling

1¾ cups flour
⅔ cup firmly packed light brown sugar
2 tablespoons MAXWELL HOUSE Instant Coffee
2½ teaspoons CALUMET Baking Powder
1 teaspoon salt
2 cups POST Raisin Bran
1⅓ cups milk
1 egg, beaten
3 tablespoons PARKAY Spread Sticks, melted

1. Heat oven to 350°F.

2. Mix flour, sugar, coffee, baking powder and salt in large bowl. Mix cereal and milk in another bowl. Stir in egg and PARKAY. Add to flour mixture; stir just until moistened. Pour into greased and floured 8x4-inch loaf pan.

3. Bake 60 to 65 minutes or until toothpick inserted in center comes out clean. Cool 5 minutes; remove from pan. Cool completely on wire rack.

Makes 1 loaf.

Note: For easier slicing, wrap and store overnight.

LEMON BLUEBERRY MUFFINS

*For a lovely gift when visiting old friends, pack these muffins in a small
basket lined with a pretty cloth napkin or dish towel.*

Prep time: 20 minutes
Baking time: 20 minutes

1⅓ cups flour

½ cup sugar

1 tablespoon CALUMET Baking Powder

¼ teaspoon salt

1 egg

1 cup milk

⅓ cup margarine *or* shortening, melted

1½ teaspoons grated lemon peel

1½ cups POST BLUEBERRY MORNING Cereal

1. Heat oven to 400°F.

2. Mix flour, sugar, baking powder and salt in large bowl. Beat egg in small bowl; stir in milk, margarine and peel. Add to flour mixture; stir just until moistened. (Batter will be lumpy.)

3. Stir in cereal. Spoon batter into greased or paper-lined muffin cups, filling each cup ⅔ full.

4. Bake 20 minutes or until golden brown. Serve warm with flavored butter, if desired.

Makes 12.

Orange Blueberry Muffins: Prepare muffins as directed, substituting grated orange peel for lemon peel.

FESTIVE FINISHES

Your holiday appetizers, main and side dishes and desserts will gain even greater appeal when you dress them up with these simple but spectacular garnishes. Add a drizzle of chocolate, twist of lemon, flourish of edible flowers or any of our other cheery trims to your foods to turn them into eye-catching presentations.

DESSERT DECORATIONS

CHOCOLATE CURLS

Encircle a pie or cake with a border of small chocolate curls. Or add just a few chocolate curls to an individual serving of pudding or mousse.

To make them, melt 4 squares of BAKER'S Semi-Sweet Chocolate (directions, page 58). Using a spatula, spread the melted chocolate into a very thin layer on a cookie sheet. Refrigerate it about 10 minutes or until firm, but still pliable. Slip the tip of a straight-edge metal spatula under the chocolate, then firmly push the spatula under to create the curl. If the chocolate is too firm to curl, let it stand a few minutes at room temperature; refrigerate it again if it becomes too soft.

Using a toothpick, carefully pick up the chocolate curls and set them on a wax paper-lined cookie sheet. Refrigerate them about 15 minutes or until firm. To arrange the curls, use toothpicks to lift and place them on desserts. Refrigerate until ready to serve.

Chocolate Curls

CHOCOLATE CUTOUTS

Embellish frosted cakes by placing chocolate cutouts on the tops or sides. Melt 4 squares of BAKER'S Semi-Sweet Chocolate (directions, page 58). Pour the chocolate onto a wax paper-lined cookie sheet; use a spatula to spread it to a ⅛-inch thickness. Refrigerate it about 15 minutes or until firm. Using cookie cutters, cut shapes from the chocolate. Immediately lift the shapes from the wax paper with a spatula or knife, then refrigerate them until you're ready to decorate.

Chocolate Cutouts

CHOCOLATE DRIZZLES

Place 1 square of BAKER'S Semi-Sweet Chocolate in a freezer zipper-style plastic sandwich bag; close the bag tightly. Microwave on HIGH about 1 minute or until the chocolate is melted. Fold down the top of the bag tightly and snip a tiny (about ⅛-inch) piece off the corner. Holding the top of the bag firmly, drizzle the chocolate through the opening to add elegance to brownies, cookies, cakes or desserts.

Chocolate Drizzles

DESSERT DECORATIONS (CONTINUED)

DIPPED FRUITS AND NUTS

Crown individual pieces of dessert with a dollop of COOL WHIP Whipped Topping and a chocolate-dipped nut or piece of fruit. To dip nuts or fruit, melt BAKER'S Semi-Sweet Chocolate or BAKER'S GERMAN'S Sweet Chocolate (directions, page 58). Dip fruit or nuts into the chocolate and let the excess drip off. Then let the dipped fruit or nuts stand, or refrigerate them on a wax paper-lined tray, about 30 minutes or until the chocolate is firm. For double-dip fruit or nuts, first dip the fruit or nut in melted BAKER'S Premium White Chocolate; let it stand to dry. Then dip it in melted semi-sweet chocolate.

Dipped Fruits and Nuts

CHOCOLATE LEAVES

Use nontoxic leaves, such as mint, lemon or strawberry, and melted BAKER'S Semi-Sweet Chocolate (directions, page 58). With a small paintbrush, spread several coats of melted chocolate on the underside of each leaf. Wipe off any chocolate on the top side of the leaf. Then place the leaves, chocolate side up, on a wax paper-lined baking sheet or a curved surface such as a rolling pin; refrigerate until the chocolate is firm. Before using, peel the leaf away from the chocolate.

Chocolate Leaves

TOASTED NUTS AND COCONUT

For your favorite pudding dessert or frosted cakes or cookies, add a sprinkling of toasted nuts or coconut evenly or in a pattern across the top, around the edge or on each serving. To toast nuts or coconut, spread them in a thin layer on a shallow baking pan. Bake them in a 350°F oven 5 to 10 minutes or until golden brown, stirring once or twice. If you like, toast extra to freeze for future desserts.

Toasted Nuts and Coconut

EDIBLE FLOWER BOUQUETS

Whether you use the whole blossom or just snip the petals, edible flowers make easy, elegant garnishes. Especially good with sweets are pansies, violets, rose petals, dianthus and daylilies. Other favorites include marigold, viola, nasturtium, chamomile and rosemary. Not all flowers are edible, so contact your local poison control center, restaurant suppliers or herb growers for advice on available flowers that are safe to use.

Edible Flower Bouquets

VEGETABLE AND FRUIT GARNISHES

ONION BRUSHES

To enhance any main dish, make an onion brush garnish by slicing off the root end of a green onion and trimming most of the top portion. With a sharp paring knife, make slashes at both ends to produce a fringe. Then place the onion in a bowl of ice-cold water so the ends curl back to resemble brushes.

DECORATIVE CUTOUTS

Add colorful cutouts to the top of a casserole, on a plate with appetizers or in a salad. Use a star, moon, heart or other shape of aspic cutter or hors d'oeuvre cutter to make shapes from strips of sweet red, orange, yellow, purple or green pepper. Or, if you wish, peel an orange, lemon or lime, then cut shapes from the peel.

CITRUS TWISTS

Add extra color and variety to salads and desserts with lemon, orange and lime twists. Use a sharp knife to cut your fruit into ⅛-inch-thick slices. Then cut from the outside edge to the center of each slice, and twist the ends in opposite directions.

FRUIT FANS

One of the easiest and prettiest of all fruit garnishes is a strawberry fan, a perfect complement for desserts and salads. To make a fan, place a strawberry, hull-side down, on a cutting board. Make narrow lengthwise cuts, being careful not to slice all the way to the other end. Then hold the strawberry gently in one hand and twist it with the other, fanning out the slices. For larger fruit fans, try using oranges, lemons and limes. Cut the fruit lengthwise into quarters. Then slice and fan out each quarter as for the strawberries.

FRESH HERBS

Fresh herbs can add a simple and elegant touch that is appealing as well as appetizing. To garnish dips, spreads and plates of appetizers, add sprigs of tarragon, dill, thyme, cilantro or rosemary. You also can add a sprig of fresh mint to a dessert or sprinkle fresh thyme or sage leaves on a main dish.

Onion Brushes

Decorative Cutouts

Citrus Twists

Fruit Fans

EXTRA HOLIDAY
MAIN DISHES

Turn any day into a
memorable occasion with
these scrumptious chicken
dishes from Kraft Foods.
Whether you need a
fabulous but fast meal for
company on a busy
weeknight or an extra
entrée at your holiday feast,
here are six easy recipes
that'll fit the bill.

QUICK HOLIDAY CHICKEN STIR-FRY

*When you're REALLY short on time, use frozen mixed
vegetables in this Oriental dish for a shortcut.*

Prep time: 10 minutes
Cooking time: 7 minutes

½ cup MIRACLE WHIP *or* MIRACLE WHIP LIGHT Dressing,
   divided

4 boneless skinless chicken breast halves (about
   1¼ pounds), cut into thin strips

¼ to ½ teaspoon garlic powder

3 cups assorted fresh cut-up vegetables *or* 1 package
   (16 ounces) frozen mixed vegetables

2 tablespoons soy sauce

2 cups hot cooked MINUTE Original Rice

1. Heat 2 tablespoons of the dressing in skillet on
medium-high heat. Add chicken and garlic powder;
stir-fry 3 minutes.

2. Add vegetables; stir-fry 3 minutes or until chicken is cooked through. Reduce heat to medium.

3. Stir in remaining dressing and soy sauce; simmer 1 minute. Serve over rice.

Makes 4 servings.

PARTY CHICKEN KABOBS

*Marinate the chicken ahead of time, then put these kabobs under the broiler
for a light meal. Keep it simple with a tossed salad and a side of rice.*

Prep time: 20 minutes plus marinating
Broiling OR grilling time: 20 minutes

3 cups KRAFT CATALINA French Dressing *or*
   KRAFT CATALINA FREE Fat Free Dressing

2 to 3 pounds boneless skinless chicken breast halves,
   cubed

   Assorted cut-up fresh vegetables

   Hot cooked MINUTE Original Rice

1. Pour dressing over chicken and vegetables; cover.
Refrigerate several hours or overnight to marinate.
Drain; discard marinade. Heat broiler or grill.

2. Arrange chicken and vegetables alternately on
8 to 10 skewers. Place skewers on rack of broiler

pan 5 to 7 inches from heat or on greased grill over
medium coals.

3. Broil or grill, covered, 8 to 10 minutes on
each side or until chicken is cooked through. Serve
over rice.

Makes 8 to 10 servings.

Quick Holiday Chicken Stir-Fry

BAKED HONEY DIJON CHICKEN BREASTS

Mix KRAFT Honey Dijon Dressing with soy sauce for an effortless, yet succulent, sauce for these chicken breasts.

Prep time: 5 minutes
Baking time: 30 minutes

   4 boneless skinless chicken breast halves (about 1¼ pounds)
   1 bottle (8 ounces) KRAFT Honey Dijon Dressing
 ¼ cup soy sauce

1. Heat oven to 400°F.

2. Place chicken in 13x9-inch baking dish. Mix dressing and soy sauce. Pour over chicken.

3. Bake 30 minutes or until chicken is cooked through.

Makes 4 servings.

PARMESAN CHICKEN BREASTS

Here's a no-fry chicken that has a crunchy crust, thanks to the tasty Parmesan-bread coating.

Prep time: 10 minutes
Baking time: 25 minutes

 ½ cup (2 ounces) KRAFT 100% Grated Parmesan Cheese
 ¼ cup dry bread crumbs
   1 teaspoon *each* dried oregano leaves and parsley flakes
 ¼ teaspoon *each* paprika, salt and black pepper
   6 boneless skinless chicken breast halves (about 2 pounds)
   2 tablespoons PARKAY Spread Sticks, melted

1. Heat oven to 400°F. Spray 15x10x1-inch baking pan with no stick cooking spray.

2. Mix cheese, crumbs and seasonings. Dip chicken in PARKAY; coat with cheese mixture. Place in prepared pan.

3. Bake 20 to 25 minutes or until cooked through.

Makes 6 servings.

Spicy Parmesan Chicken Breasts: Substitute ⅛ to ¼ teaspoon ground red pepper for black pepper.

SWISS 'N' CHICKEN CASSEROLE

Hot and hearty, this casserole resembles a hot chicken salad. It's ideal for bringing to a family or church potluck dinner.

Prep time: 20 minutes
Baking time: 40 minutes

- 4 cups chopped cooked chicken
- 2 cups (8 ounces) shredded KRAFT Natural Swiss Cheese
- 2 cups croutons
- 2 cups sliced celery
- 1 cup MIRACLE WHIP *or* MIRACLE WHIP LIGHT Dressing
- ½ cup milk
- ¼ cup chopped onion
- 1 teaspoon salt
- ⅛ teaspoon pepper
- ¼ cup chopped walnuts, toasted

1. Heat oven to 350°F.

2. Mix all ingredients except walnuts. Spoon into 2-quart casserole; sprinkle with walnuts.

3. Bake 40 minutes or until thoroughly heated. Garnish with green onion and carrot curls.

Makes 6 servings.

CHEESY CHICKEN CASSEROLE

Here's a delicious way to use up your holiday chicken or turkey. Your family will never guess that they're eating leftovers.

Prep time: 15 minutes
Baking time: 30 minutes

- 1½ cups (6 ounces) KRAFT Natural Shredded Sharp Cheddar Cheese, divided
- 1½ cups chopped cooked chicken *or* turkey
- 1½ cups (4 ounces) bow tie pasta, cooked, drained
- 1 package (10 ounces) frozen chopped broccoli, thawed, drained
- ½ cup KRAFT Real Mayonnaise
- ½ cup chopped green *or* red pepper
- ¼ cup milk
- ½ teaspoon *each* crushed dried oregano leaves and garlic salt
- ¾ cup seasoned croutons (optional)

1. Heat oven to 350°F.

2. Mix all ingredients except ½ cup of the cheese and the croutons.

3. Spoon into 1½-quart casserole. Sprinkle with reserved ½ cup cheese and croutons.

4. Bake 30 minutes or until thoroughly heated. Garnish with red pepper rings and fresh parsley.

Makes 4 to 6 servings.

'TIS THE SEASON FOR CELEBRATIONS

Holiday entertaining is now simpler than ever before with our special selection of eight preplanned party menus. Using the recipes from this book, you can easily share the spirit of the season with friends and family at a Co-Host Thanksgiving Dinner, Bowl Game Bash, Gala New Year's Celebration and many more festive events.

CO-HOST THANKSGIVING DINNER

Share the cooking with others, using this potluck menu, so you can share in the fun.

Ranch Dip with crudités (recipe, page 9)
Roasted turkey
Sausage Stuffing (recipe, page 30)
Classic Green Bean Casserole (recipe, page 39)
Cranberry Cream Cheese Mold (recipe, page 38)
Double Layer Pumpkin Pie (recipe, page 51)

PIZZA PARTY FOR SANTA'S HELPERS

Here's a holiday party created just for kids.

Party Pizza Appetizers (recipe, page 17)
Italian Vegetable Dip with cut-up vegetables (recipe, page 11)
Parmesan Breadstick Candy Canes (recipe, page 80)
JIGGLERS® Holiday Time Gelatin (recipe, page 65)
Individual Chocolate Pizzas (recipe, page 72)

COOKIE AND CANDY EXCHANGE

*Invite the guests, set out the sweets and provide the holiday tins so each
guest can select their assortment of holiday cookies and candies.*

PHILLY® Cream Cheese Cookies (recipe, page 77)
Kris Kringle Cookies (recipe, page 75)
Chocolate Cherry Thumbprint Cookies (recipe, page 78)
ONE BOWL® Chocolate Fudge (recipe, page 69)
Crispy Marshmallow Tree (recipe, page 70)
Holiday Peppermint Candies (recipe, page 73)

A FESTIVAL OF LIGHTS

*No last-minute prep required for this traditional Hanukkah meal. The
salad and dessert can be made ahead of time, and the beef and potatoes
will cook in the oven while you're enjoying your guests.*

Brisket of beef
Herb-Roasted Potatoes (recipe, page 32)
Steamed Carrots
Assorted dinner rolls
Snowflake Macaroons (recipe, page 78)

*Three dishes from Co-Host Thanksgiving Dinner: Cranberry Cream
Cheese Mold, Sausage Stuffing, Classic Green Bean Casserole*

JOYFUL CHRISTMAS BRUNCH

*Ah, the magic of Christmas morning—gifts to open, stockings to empty
and this special holiday brunch to share.*

Bacon Breakfast Casserole (recipe, page 37)
OSCAR MAYER® Little Smokies
Greens with Pear and Pecan (recipe, page 39) *or* fresh fruit bowl
Cape Cod Blueberry Cake (recipe, page 54)

BUON APPETITO ITALIAN FAMILY SUPPER

Gather your family around the table to feast on this holiday dinner.

Carbonara Appetizers (recipe, page 17)
Parmesan Chicken Breasts (recipe, page 88)
Italian Pasta Salad (recipe, page 40)
Tossed greens with KRAFT® Zesty Italian Dressing
Cheesy Biscuits (recipe, page 43)
Holiday Poke Cake (recipe, page 49)

GALA NEW YEAR'S CELEBRATION

Ring in the new year in style with this elegant appetizer-and-dessert party.

Hot Artichoke Dip with toasted French bread slices (recipe, page 14)
Party Cheese Wreath with assorted crackers (recipe, page 19)
Quick Crabmeat Appetizer (recipe, page 20)
Bacon Water Chestnuts (recipe, page 24)
Little Tacos (recipe, page 26)
Heavenly Chocolate Cake (recipe, page 52)
PHILLY 3-STEP™ Caramel Pecan Cheesecake (recipe, page 57)
Easy Chocolate Holiday Dessert (recipe, page 60)

BOWL GAME BASH

Here are seven super snacks and sweets to serve at your next Super Bowl party.

Shredded Wheat Party Mix (recipe, page 6)
VELVEETA® Salsa Dip with cut-up vegetables (recipe, page 13)
PHILLY® 7-Layer Mexican Dip with tortilla chips (recipe, page 16)
Little Gems (recipe, page 25)
CATALINA® Chicken Wings with blue cheese dressing (recipe, page 26)
ONE BOWL® Brownies (recipe, page 59)
Chewy Caramel Bars (recipe, page 73)

D–O

METRIC CHART

METRIC COOKING HINTS

By making a few conversions, cooks in Australia, Canada, and the United Kingdom can use the recipes in *Holiday Homecoming*™ with confidence. The charts on this page provide a guide for converting measurements from the U.S. customary system, which is used throughout this book, to the imperial and metric systems. There also is a conversion table for oven temperatures to accommodate the differences in oven calibrations.

Product Differences: Most of the ingredients called for in the recipes in this book are available in English-speaking countries. However, some are known by different names. Here are some common American ingredients and their possible counterparts:
- Sugar is granulated or castor sugar.
- Powdered sugar is icing sugar.
- All-purpose flour is plain household flour or white flour. When self-rising flour is used in place of all-purpose flour in a recipe that calls for leavening, omit the leavening agent (baking soda or baking powder) and salt.
- Light-colored corn syrup is golden syrup.
- Cornstarch is cornflour.
- Baking soda is bicarbonate of soda.
- Vanilla is vanilla essence.
- Green, red or yellow sweet peppers are capsicums.
- Golden raisins are sultanas.

Volume and Weight: Americans traditionally use cup measures for liquid and solid ingredients. The chart, above right, shows the approximate imperial and metric equivalents. If you are accustomed to weighing solid ingredients, the following approximate equivalents will be helpful.
- 1 cup butter, castor sugar, or rice = 8 ounces = about 250 grams
- 1 cup flour = 4 ounces = about 125 grams
- 1 cup icing sugar = 5 ounces = about 150 grams

Spoon measures are used for smaller amounts of ingredients. Although the size of the tablespoon varies slightly in different countries, for practical purposes and for recipes in this book, a straight substitution is all that's necessary.

Measurements made using cups or spoons always should be level unless stated otherwise.

EQUIVALENTS: U.S. / AUSTRALIA/U.K.

⅛ teaspoon = 0.5 ml
¼ teaspoon = 1 ml
½ teaspoon = 2 ml
1 teaspoon = 5 ml
1 tablespoon = 1 tablespoon
¼ cup = 2 tablespoons = 2 fluid ounces = 60 ml
⅓ cup = ¼ cup = 3 fluid ounces = 90 ml
½ cup = ⅓ cup = 4 fluid ounces = 120 ml
⅔ cup = ½ cup = 5 fluid ounces = 150 ml
¾ cup = ⅔ cup = 6 fluid ounces = 180 ml
1 cup = ¾ cup = 8 fluid ounces = 240 ml
1¼ cups = 1 cup
2 cups = 1 pint
1 quart = 1 litre
½ inch = 1.27 cm
1 inch = 2.54 cm

BAKING PAN SIZES

American	Metric
8x1½-inch round baking pan	20x4-centimeter cake tin
9x1½-inch round baking pan	23x3.5-centimeter cake tin
11x7x1½-inch baking pan	28x18x4-centimeter baking tin
13x9x2-inch baking pan	30x20x3-centimeter baking tin
2-quart rectangular baking dish	30x20x3-centimeter baking tin
15x10x1-inch baking pan (Swiss roll tin)	30x25x2-centimeter baking tin (Swiss roll tin)
9-inch pie plate	22x4- or 23x4-centimeter pie plate
7- or 8-inch springform pan	18- or 20-centimeter springform or loose-bottom cake tin
9x5x3-inch loaf pan	23x13x7-centimeter or 2-pound narrow loaf tin or pâté tin
1½-quart casserole	1.5-litre casserole
2-quart casserole	2-litre casserole

OVEN TEMPERATURE EQUIVALENTS

Fahrenheit Setting	Celsius Setting*	Gas Setting
300°F	150°C	Gas Mark 2 (slow)
325°F	160°C	Gas Mark 3 (moderately slow)
350°F	180°C	Gas Mark 4 (moderate)
375°F	190°C	Gas Mark 5 (moderately hot)
400°F	200°C	Gas Mark 6 (hot)
425°F	220°C	Gas Mark 7
450°F	230°C	Gas Mark 8 (very hot)
Broil		Grill

* Electric and gas ovens may be calibrated using Celsius. However, for an electric oven, increase the Celsius setting 10 to 20 degrees when cooking above 160°C. For convection or forced-air ovens (gas or electric), lower the temperature setting 10°C when cooking at all heat levels.

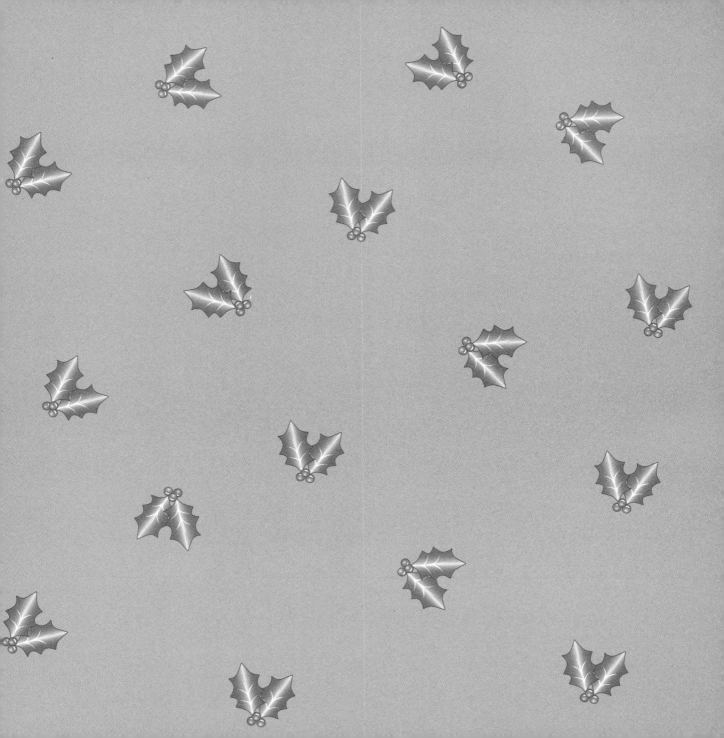